Dr. Winston R. Dykeman,
P. O. Box 67,
Hillsborough, N. B.
E0A 1X0

Second-Mile People

Isobel Kuhn

OMF BOOKS

Copyright © OVERSEAS MISSIONARY
FELLOWSHIP

First published .... *June 1982*
Reprinted .... *April 1983*

ISBN 0 85363 145 X

*Published by Overseas Missionary Fellowship, Belmont, The Vine,
Sevenoaks, Kent, TN13 3TZ
Printed in Great Britain by Richard Clay (The Chaucer Press)
Ltd, Bungay, Suffolk. Typesetting by Bookmag, Henderson Road,
Inverness.*

CONTENTS

FOREWORD

SOME MONTHS AGO I was looking for something in our archives room in Sevenoaks, when I saw a box labelled, among other things, KUHN. Being of an inquisitive nature I opened it and, to my great surprise, found it contained a manuscript I had never seen before. My original quest forgotten, I sat spellbound reading it, unable at first to believe I had really found an unpublished manuscript by Isobel Kuhn. The style, however, is unmistakably hers, and it was accompanied by a letter dated May 8th 1939 from her to Mr Baker, then OMF Editorial Secretary; this implies that *Precious Things of the Lasting Hills*, her first book, had recently been published and that she was thinking about further writing based on her circular letters. *Comrades of the Second Mile* (her original title for this book) had evidently been sent the year before, for she writes, 'Your letter written August 1938 came in February (!)

. . . It is very kind of you to take time from busy days to set my heart at rest about the arrival of *Comrades*.'

Why should a book written so long ago and dealing with situations long since changed now be published for the first time? Those of us who have read it feel that the spiritual teaching contained in these chapters is of timeless relevance, and has a message for the 1980s as much as for the 1930s. The six colleagues of whom Isobel Kuhn writes were those who stood out for her as 'lights out of the night', as she puts it in the prologue. 'They have shone across our "first mile" pathway as splendid meteors trailing such radiance after them that something of their own celestial fire has sought to enter into us also.'

Some of this material will be familiar to those who have read other Kuhn books, particularly *By Searching*, and it need be no secret that 'Bachelor' is J O Fraser who had such an influence on Isobel's life. Let the others remain anonymous, as she meant them to be — examples to us all in being 'Second-Mile People'.

Edyth A Banks, Editor

PROLOGUE

THE GREATEST PEACE LOVER this world has ever
seen, once said, 'Whosoever shall compel thee to
go a mile, go with him twain.' (Matt. 5:41). There
were probably many who listened to Him that
spring day on the mount in Galilee, who turned
away with a smile at the thought of such a 'ridiculous' doctrine! But that SECOND MILE was too
vividly new an idea to this earth, and it has
strangely clung to human hearts all down the
centuries. Gradually, in common thought, it has
seemed to slip from its setting and, so to speak,
become opalescent with a variety of shades of the
original meaning all more or less coloured with
the thought of voluntary sacrifice.

It is as this 'unset' stone that we use it in these
sketches. We look at it apart from any doctrinal
teaching, and as we turn it over in our thoughts as
one turns an opal in the palm of his hand, we see
the flame-colour of sacrificial offering shoot from
its still surface. Christ made a difference between
that first and second mile. He says plainly the first
was *compulsory*, but He puts the second up to you
and me as *His* way of doing it — in other words He

7

suggests it as an offering that you and I may bring for the good and the peace of His kingdom.

Today one finds a general apathy in the church, an unspoken feeling that one mile for the Saviour is quite sufficient! The writer has more than once heard this remark, 'I am afraid to yield myself wholly up to Christ . . . afraid of what He might ask me to give up, or to do!' There seems to be a fear of that '*second mile*'.

But all in our generation are not so diffident. In fact, occasionally we have touched lives with an absolutely different point of view; lives that cried out, not 'How much will He ask?' but 'How much *can I give Him?*'; young hearts that have rung with gratitude, 'All this for me? All this for me?' These have been as 'lights out of the night that flashed'. They have shone across our 'first mile' pathway as splendid meteors trailing such radiance after them that something of their own 'celestial fire' has sought to enter into us also.

We introduce these selected few to you, more or less in the order in which God brought them on to our own horizons.

1

BACHELOR — A 'LOST' LIFE

'FOR WHOSOEVER WOULD SAVE *his life shall lose it; but whosoever shall lose his life for My sake, the same shall save it' (Luke 9:24)*. It was only my second summer conference in a wooded spot by the borders of a mirror lake. Wanting something from the living room I rushed impetuously in, then found myself facing a gentleman, tall and slightly bald, who was sitting there quietly. (I did not take time to see what he was doing!) Something about him made me say to myself, 'Oh! . . . some old bachelor or other!' and with all a young girl's horror of such, I as quickly rushed out again.

Not another thought was given to this stranger till evening fell, and the happy group gathered in the spicy air of the auditorium, which is a cleared glade among the fir trees. It was the opening session of the conference and I got settled in among the other girls before I inspected the platform, but when I did lift my eyes, I got a shock. Why, there was that bachelor fellow sitting in the Speaker's chair! Surely *he* wasn't to be a conference leader? Was he who had looked so . . . well . . . uncared for, going to turn out to be somebody

9

important? The chairman was introducing him
before I knew it, and a few minutes later Mr
Bachelor was talking to us in a quiet but resonant
voice. He said he was a tribes worker in far
western China. He had gone to the mission field
rather young (at 22 years of age) and was there for
fourteen years before a furlough. The aboriginal
tribe called 'Lisu', among whom he spent the most
of that time, had no language in writing, and he
proposed to take us on mental tours each night,
through various phases of his work among these
interesting people. One evening he would devote
to telling how he put their language into writing,
one to their customs, one to stories of life amongst
them etc. This evening he wished to take us on a
visit through their homes and villages.

From the first this tall missionary held one's
attention, for there was something commanding
about his address, despite its simplicity; but when
he began to describe his dearly loved mountain
fastnesses and their native children, he quite lost
himself, and his audience went with him! Each
evening we left the murmuring pine-boughs, the
rustic platform, the twinkle of electric lights here
and there in the foliage, and were transported in a
second to far China to go wandering up and down
on entrancing excursions in Lisuland with Bachelor as guide.

I remember one such time crossing a great river
which cuts its way in serpentine coils through the
rocky feet of a mighty mountain range. We could
feel the precarious tip of the bamboo raft we stood
upon, as the swift and dangerous current swung it

partially around from time to time; what a relief
when the steep bank was finally reached! Then
started the difficult ascent. The sun beat mer-
cilessly upon our backs, the gravelly pebbles of the
simple cow-path slipped beneath our feet, and all
the time we felt clutching after us the clammy
fever-smiting fingers of the malarial vapours
which make that river bed a bed of death to many
a traveller, and which the Chinese call the 'poison
mist'.

What gladness when one has managed the first
five hundred feet and stands upon a jutting rock,
hats off, arms outspread to catch the welcome cold
mountain breeze that whips against our hot weary
bodies with all the zip and tang of a cold shower
bath. 'Oh-oh' — (sigh of deep gratitude) 'Thank
the Lord for travelling mercies! What! Bachelor
says we have only climbed about a third of the
way? Ai-ya! Well, let us stretch out a minute on
that grassy nob, and relax; tell that grinning Lisu
boy who is carrying your bedding on his back,
Bachelor, that it is all very well for him to smile,
but foreign backs and legs are not trained to these
precipitous hillsides from babyhood like his were!
Ah, how beautiful that high jagged peak is yonder,
with the soft little white cloud cuddled round its
neck . . . looks like a scarf of chiffon draped around
a proud Court Beauty's shoulders. All right! All
right! I'll get up . . . ugh, those tired muscles. Here
we are — on with you!'

So one travels on, hour after hour; there is no
lunch place but about two o'clock we might see
ahead of us a few rickety-looking shacks tilted

against the mountain side. As there are practically no level spots on the side of the ranges that border the Salween river, Lisu houses seldom rest entirely on the ground; to get their floors level they build on poles of varying lengths (according to the distance out from the hillside) and so their homes look like ragged boys on stilts! It gives one a 'suspended-in-the-air' feeling to stand in the doorway of one such, and see Mother Earth drop away from underneath you in a kind of monstrous toboggan slide of hundreds of feet.

One such hamlet, said Bachelor, was named Mock-Turtle village, and as we approach in sight the missionary sends a ringing 'halloo' up the steep path ahead — 'Ma-pa is coming' (In Lisuland the male teacher is called Ma-pa and the female, Ma-ma.)

In a second out rush an army of dogs —

'Hark, hark! the dogs do bark!
Strangers are coming to Lisutown!'

People pour out of the houses and shouts of welcome and joy rend the air. As you approach (especially if it is the Christmas festival) gunshots shatter the other noises into silence and boom in echoes down the mountain sides like bounding bomb shells. A long line of Lisu wait to shake hands, and they are singing.

'There's a stranger at the door,
Let him in! Let him in!'

Punctuated with gunbursts it sounds rather more like,

'There's a stranger at the door,
Shoot him down! Shoot him down!' says

Bachelor with a chuckle.

However there is nothing but joyous welcome written on the radiant faces, and brown Lisu hands are thrust forward to shake yours. Oh, this hand-shaking in Lisuland! (It is the token of church fellowship.) Down the line you go, hot hands, cold hands, dry hands, wet hands, lean hands, fat hands, hands that grip heartily till you wince, hands that lie limply like dead fish and are worse than any other kind! Even baby strapped on mother's back must not be overlooked, and his is the only really soft hand in the line . . . for Lisu lives are only sustained by vigorous manual labour; even young girls go out daily to chop and bring in their own supply of firewood.

And then the eggs! Lisu hearts are deep and generous and they always want to give, and as everyone knows Ma-pa likes to eat eggs, in almost every hand there will be an unsuspected egg! So Bachelor says he always wears an 'egg bag' over his shoulder, and thus he goes down the line. Shake. Egg? — into bag. Shake. Egg? — into bag! and so on. And speaking of eggs, I must digress a moment.

Do not let anyone think a Spirit-filled life such as Bachelor's is a very dry affair. No, indeed, it is the only 'abundant' life, the life Christ promised when He said, 'I have come that they may have life, and may have it in abundance'.

Bachelor has a keen sense of humour . . . indeed he told us young folk it would be a tragic thing to come to the mission field without it! In describing his experiences he soon discovered that certain portions were horribly thrilling to the female part of his audience, and I am quite sure he mischievously enjoyed bringing in details just in order to hear the audible female shiver. I remember once, in speaking of the scarcity of meat and the small variety of food in those wild and barren mountain fastnesses, the casual way in which he said he went for weeks without tasting meat — 'However, once I had boiled rat'.

Among the young folk were quite a few who were themselves hoping to go to China as missionaries (five of us are at this very moment on the field). Bachelor gave himself unstintingly to this group; he taught deep spiritual truths, or discussed the life and customs of the people, or sometimes brought the darker side of missionary life forward, in order to discourage any who were merely seeking romance. Off and on his humour would gleam out in droll fashion, as once when talking with me he drawled,

'Have you ever eaten a bad egg?'

'No-o,' I shuddered, horribly fascinated at such missionary martyrdom.

'Oh' — casually — 'it's not bad, r-e-a-l-l-y.'

Long years afterwards, when I finally got to China, Bachelor himself was also a guest at my first real Chinese-invited feast. As that favourite dish of China — ancient pickled eggs — was laid on the tables, Bachelor leaned forward, with a naughty grin picked up a big shell-encrusted slice with his chopsticks, and said, 'Won't you have some?' He would have succeeded in getting me to swallow a piece (for being quite a newcomer I did not know if it were possible to refuse anything and not offend one's host) when another guest, an older lady missionary, came to my rescue, saying, 'Here — it is not necessary — don't let him tease you!' whereupon Bachelor ate it himself with a quite unnecessary display of its lusciousness!

But to return to Mock-Turtle Village. All day long adults and children are out chopping wood or farming their steep mountain plots, so evening is the time for study. Ma-pa's visits could only be so rare (he said even with travelling to different places all the time he scarcely covered his parish in one year) that probably everything would be laid aside and a short term Bible School held. Lisu build their own chapels, and often next to it they make a little room for Ma-pa which is styled 'The Prophet's Chamber'.

My husband John and I have slept in one of these. It was a tiny room in a village so many thousands of feet up in the air that it seemed very near heaven; and perhaps that is the reason its people are the sweetest and dearest group of Lisu we have ever met. A curved bamboo matting placed on end and tied to slim pillars was the wall of our chamber; large shingles merely laid (not nailed, for Lisuland knows no such luxury as nails!) on poles were the roof; two huge broad slabs of wood laid on posts driven into the ground (the 'carpet' there is Mother Earth's own brown face!) were pointed out as our beds; a long thick narrow slab on posts was our 'bureau', and when dusk fell we perceived the purpose of a large soot-marked stone, or rock, placed in the middle of the 'bureau' — it was our unsuspected lamp stand! Pine chips placed on this stone and lit not only provided light, but sent forth a pleasing aromatic odour. Altogether we spent a most happy night in that rough-hewn little 'prophet's chamber', and never in our lives have we had more loving hospitable hosts than those dear Lisu.

Bachelor told us how patience was needed in teaching these warm-hearted but long neglected aborigines. He would begin with the first question in their catechism, 'Who created the world and all that is in it?' After drilling and repeating and explaining, patiently and clearly, what this meant, and what it included, he would close the book and say — perhaps to an old Lisu mother —

'Now Mother, do you see that tree out there?'

'Yes.'

'Well — who made it?'

A look of blankness and then an engaging grin, and the happy unconcerned 'I don't know, Ma-pa!'

'Well then listen and I will tell you. GOD made it. God made everything in this 'world — the mountains, and the clouds, the river and the rocks, and trees and man. Now listen, Mother — who made that tree out there?'

Another drop-jaw look of emptiness, then the grin and 'Don't know, Ma-pa!'

'Well now, *listen* Mother, and use your mind. Put your thoughts on to it!'

'Oh there's no use, Ma-pa. I'm old, I can't remember. You go ahead and teach the youngsters! I haven't got any memory. You mustn't worry about me.'

'Mother, how many children do you have?'

'Six, Ma-pa. There's Peter over yonder, and Mary, and John who is the baby and three are dead.'

'Oh I'm sorry to hear you have lost three. Was it long ago?'

'Yes, our eldest boy was the first to go. It was four years ago in the rainy season. He was out minding the cows and a rock got loose in the cliff above and came tumbling down and hit him before he had time to jump. The rock was as big as a table. There were lots of rocks fell that summer. Why I remember . . .'

'Say Mother, I thought you said just now you couldn't remember? And here you are telling me what happened four years ago! And you remember it as well as if it were yesterday. Now Mother you *have* got a memory, and God wants you to use it. Now I want you to remember that *God* made that tree out yonder and every other tree . . .' and so on, never tiring, never getting vexed, never failing to love. And gradually his Lisu learned.

They also learned to sing. Conference was half over before I accidentally discovered that Bachelor was no mean musician. Trained by one of London's best masters, with a brilliant intellect that photographed page after page of whole symphonies and sonatas, he was 'buried' in his Lisu hills with only a portable organ for nine years, and yet when he came out, with a little brushing up he was capable of giving concerts all by himself.

One does not 'discover' a person like Bachelor

all at once. Some people seem to wear an inventory of their accomplishments hung around their neck; you are not in their presence two hours but you have learned how many university degrees they have, what honours they won, how many 'world lights' are their best friends etc etc. But that is not so with the life that is hidden in Christ. It is truly 'hidden' — if you wish to see it, you must patiently search and seek it out. It was quite some time later before I even knew that Bachelor was a science graduate of London University, and it was years before I discovered that anyone else in the world considered him a great man — a 'coming' man in the missionary realm: his references to himself were rare but always of the humblest, a simple humility that threw one off one's guard by its honesty. Christ had 'increased' so that Bachelor had forgotten just how far (as the world would review it)) he himself had 'decreased'.

So his Lisu were taught to sing in parts, and Bachelor afffirmed that he had never heard congregational singing that could touch theirs. This book is being written from a native shanty in Lisuland itself, and only the other night as a group of these children of the hills were in for a visit, they gathered around the baby organ and sang the Lisu translation of

'Hallelujah! 'tis done;
I believe on the Son;
I am saved by the blood of the Crucified One!'

As the song gathered volume the room seemed flowing with waves of wonderful melody until we were bathed, drowned, in the beauty of it. Tenor, bass, alto, soprano flowed together into one exquisite harmony, and sung from hearts that believed and loved Him wholly. The music of it was so marvellous that John and I were thrilled through and through. One of the singers had been imprisoned for Jesus' sake, another had been beaten for that same dear Name, and almost all had suffered some persecution. We understood then why Bachelor boasted of his Lisu's singing — it is set on fire, made living, by joyous faith in the truth of the words of their hymns.

The days of Conference fled quickly and soon it was the last evening: the last message had been given, and we were supposed to retire. But hearts had been made tender during those days and almost with mutual consent we gathered in the sitting room of the bungalow. I can see it now, the room lit by the crackling pine logs in the big fireplace, the older people in chairs, we younger ones seated on the floor; we overflowed, and finally when Bachelor was asked to say 'a last word' he had to stand up in the doorway, so that those outside as well as those inside might hear. Tears were in many eyes as he stood there in his tall brilliant manhood — for was he not carrying all those splendid gifts, those rare educational privileges which only Culture can 'appreciate', that strong sterling manhood, and going to bury them alive in wild mountain fastnesses where there were none even to *know* how much talent and intellectual lustre was being 'wasted' on them?

Such feeling was in the air, and Bachelor must

have felt it. He quoted simply, 'If any man will come after Me, let him deny himself, and take up his cross daily, and follow Me. For whosoever will save his life shall lose it; but whosoever will lose his life for My sake, the same shall save it.' (Luke 9:23, 24) As the leaping flames cast their playing lights and shadows on his face, Bachelor stood and said earnestly, 'You must not pity me — Christ has promised, "Verily I say unto you, there is no man that hath left house, or brethren, or sisters, or mother . . . or lands, for My sake and the gospel's, but he shall receive an hundredfold now in this time . . . and in the world to come eternal life." (Mark 10:29, 30)

'There is a promise for this life — a *hundredfold* — as well as for the next,' said Bachelor with deep seriousness. 'And you who pity me, and think I am "losing" father and mother, brothers, sisters, houses, lands, do not know that already I have received the "hundredfold". On those Lisu mountains I have more than a hundredfold in fathers, mothers, brothers and sisters. I had typhoid fever among them, and there I was far away from medical aid or even friends of my own colour. I was delirious for a time, and in between delirium I would come to and find my Lisu fathers and mothers kneeling on each side of me, holding my hands and weeping and praying. For one mother's love I have gained a hundred, for one brother or sister's, many hundreds.

'Houses? Lands? Any house, any land over thousands of miles of most enchanting Alpine scenery are mine for the wishing, mine for the taking. I can travel for days, and every spot I put my foot on is mine whenever I want to take it!'

Bachelor, most of your words that night are forgotten, but *you yourself*, your strong, clean manhood, your intellectual keenness, your musical ability and many other gifts, all these laid at Christ's feet, all these 'lost' for Him — and the strong earnest tones of your voice as you attested to the 'hundredfold' already gained — will any of us ever forget *that*? How poorly the world measures loss and gain. Saving for a moment to lose for eternity; and in that moment finding that what was gained has not been worth it after all.

> 'Measure thy life by loss instead of gain;
> Not by the wine drunk, but by the wine poured forth;
> For love's strength standeth in love's sacrifice;
> And whoso suffers most hath most to give.'

There was more 'loss' awaiting Bachelor — loss that his earnest thoughtful eyes brooding into the fire that night could not foresee. But the truth of the hundredfold gain which his heart proclaimed in ringing triumph is also true, and did not fail him even although he was not allowed to 'see' it until the pain of the loss and its heart tears, had cleared from his vision.

*   *   *

Conference broke up — each to his own city. Bachelor's sailing port and my home were separated by a sea-journey. But before he left he was

asked to address the China Inland Mission friends
in my town, and he had expected to stay there as
the guest of an old friend. However, when he
landed that friend met him on the wharf with the
news that the night before his house had burned,
so he could not accommodate him! Could he think
of someone else he knew? My father had once
invited him to come and see us, so he rang up and
asked if he might come now. Of course father
replied yes, even though in his heart he feared
mother would not approve. Mother was a Christian, had been president of the Women's Missionary Society in the past, but when it came to letting
her only daughter (oh what plans she had been
making for that daughter!) go bury herself on the
mission field — that was a different question. And
upon that question she had become most hurt,
resenting any touch with Missions lest they en-
courage my 'silly romantic ideas', and especially
did she resent the China Inland Mission to which
I wished to apply. And now here was one of them
invited to live under her roof for a week!

Into such a difficult atmosphere did Bachelor
walk that summer evening. How he did it we none
of us know, but before the week was over no one in
the house was so loud in his praise as our little
mother! She declared that never had she had a
guest who was so little trouble; and his cultured
conversation . . . not a bit fanatical . . . was so
broad, why, he knew a little on every subject! And
as for his music . . . well, mother too was a musician, had composed some and had never had her
compositions refused by a publishing house, but

she declared she was ready to sit at his feet and learn. How much Bachelor quietly did to unlatch my door to China, I do not know. But I do know that this week of more intimate contact with him gave one or two opportunities for personal conversation on practical spirituality, which laid foundations in my Christian life for which I have never ceased to thank God. It was Bachelor who first taught me 'the Second Mile viewpoint', and after one has once tasted its sweetness one cannot be satisfied with less.

Although Bachelor had gently and kindly won his way into mother's heart, he was quite conscious that that heart was still steeled against the offering of her child to Christ for China. In spite of all her church enthusiasm for Missions, mother inwardly considered them 'charities' (I wonder if there are others like her?). And that her carefully-planned-for daughter should live on 'charity'! — her pride rebelled fiercely.

Before he left Bachelor gave over one morning to helping me with my problems. We walked to the ocean beach not far away and sat down to talk together in private. I knew there was persistent opposition to my 'call' to China and so I had asked Bachelor to 'analyze' it for me. But he seemed burdened that morning, and as if his own thoughts carried him away. So to make a beginning I asked him to underline a Bible verse for me to take to Moody Bible Institute, if the Lord finally opened the way to attend there. This is what he gave me — 'Casting all your care upon Him; for He careth for you. Be sober, be vigilant;

because your adversary the devil, as a roaring
lion, walketh about, seeking whom he may de-
vour. *Whom resist*', and the last words he under-
lined twice. Again he seemed abstracted, his eyes
brooding over the gay little blue wavelets as they
danced in the morning sunshine.

'You want to go to China, Isobel?'

'Yes' — the question seemed superfluous. I
wondered why he was acting so strangely, as if
depressed.

'There is great opposition. I feel your mother
will never consent to your going . . . I doubt if you
ever get there.' . . . a long pause in which the
depression passed on to me also.

Then he said, 'You are very young, aren't you?'
I told him my age.

'Yes,' he murmured — and brooded — then
roused himself and said, 'Well, if ever you get to
Moody, all will not be conquered then. Satan may
try to get you away! Your mother is not strong —
and it is quite possible that something like this
may happen. She may get ill and feel herself worse
than she is, and wire you to return immediately.
Then, perhaps if you *did* leave and come home, she
might be well enough to meet you at the station,
and your chance of Moody will be lost. How far
away is the Institute — nearly a week's journey, I
believe?'

'Yes.'

'Well, if any telegram of that sort should come, I
would advise your doing this. You would have to
take *some* time to pack your trunk and arrange for

your ticket . . . well, I would advise your wiring the nearest CIM secretary and asking for a reply as to whether the illness is really so serious or not. Perhaps a reassuring answer would arrive and save your returning home . . . in short, keep you at the Institute till you graduated.'

I pause in awe at this point, for I am walking on very sacred ground. Who knows how deeply the Spirit-filled heart dwells in Christ?

Bachelor, do you know you prophesied that summer morning? No human foresight, no matter how clever the brain, could have foreseen the chain of events that were to fall before a year was ended. And Bachelor, though he did not get the details correct, had given me just exactly the weapon with which to defeat Satan in the coming unknown days.

To prove the power of a Spirit-filled life, I will tell you what happened subsequently:

I reached Moody in September; in December a telegram was handed to me simply stating mother had died, after an operation. What I did not learn till long after was that the night before she entered the hospital she wrote something like this to an old friend far away: 'As I look back over my life, its busy church work and all, I feel that much of it has been "wood, hay and stubble". Perhaps my little girl has chosen the better part in wishing to give her all to Christ. If God will spare me after the operation tomorrow, I will try to build the "gold, silver and precious stones".' Although she never said to any of the family that she had yielded at

last in the matter of my missionary call, I always
have felt that I came to China with my mother's
blessing upon me.

Just a few weeks after that grievously shocking
telegram — it was so unexpected — a second
telegram called me out of a student class. It was
from my only brother, who at that time was very
bitter against my going to China, and it said,
'Father fatally injured, elevator accident. Return
immediately.'

After the first wild cry of sorrow — for it seemed
too much to bear on top of the first — the words of
Bachelor came to me like a flash, 'Satan may try to
get you away from Moody' — and then his very
practical advice. I told it to dear Mr Isaac Page of
the China Inland Mission, who was living in
Chicago then, and he said he would attend to the
wiring. So I quietly prepared as I could and
waited. Before evening the following telegram
came from the nearest CIM secretary, and set my
heart at rest — 'Father recovering sends love says
by no means return'. And so, as one who knows
these conflicts put it, 'Satan was sold.'

*   *   *

And now for Bachelor's 'loss'. He who had foreseen my future in such a wonderfully lucid way
was quite unprepared for his own, and that is
sometimes God's ways with His prophets. 'The
man who has no experience in the dark, has no
secret to communicate in the light' says an Indian
Sister of the Common Life. Thus Bachelor was
allowed to enter the dark.

Arriving in Shanghai filled with the thrilling hope of soon being once more among his own dear people, he was staggered by a kindly yet urgent request that he should not reurn to Lisuland but, on the contrary, fill a need at the other end of China! The one who asked was so obviously a Spirit-led man, so sympathetic in realizing what it meant, that Bachelor felt it must be the will of God. But oh, must one 'lose' one's life more than once? And how about that 'hundredfold' — must one lose it too?

Yes, there is more than one second mile in the Christian's pathway. Remember — the first mile was compulsory, 'If any man compel thee to go a mile,' but the second is only indicated, suggested, and then the Master waits for it to be offered — 'Go with him twain'; there is love in that whispered suggestion. Bachelor was not compelled to give up his Lisu, his 'hundredfold'. If he had insisted he could doubtless have returned to them, but though it tore him to pieces, he could not refuse the Second Mile when Christ so lovingly indicated it. Once before had he lost his life and found it saved a hundredfold in the affections of his Lisu brothers and sisters. Now again he was to lose it and to lose the touch with his hundredfold also.

It seemed as if he could not write to any of his conference friends for weeks after that decision; and when word did finally drift to me it seemed to be just one thought. He quoted 'Whosoever will save his life shall lose it but whosoever shall lose his life for My sake and the gospel's shall save it', and the simple comment 'God is asking me to lose my life for His sake.' Oh the heart-tears, how they blinded his vision to the second hundredfold which must surely come from this second big losing!

The memory of that second losing never fails to still my heart into awe, even now. Always at thought of it comes Bachelor's face in the firelight and the ring of his voice, 'For one mother's love I have gained a hundred, for one brother or sister's many hundreds!' Why, the Lisu were Bachelor's *life*; how *could* he endure not to return to work among them?

Five years passed before I met Bachelor again. At the beginning of those years stood Bachelor's comment, as he looked at the obstacles, 'I doubt if you ever get to China'; at the end I stood in Shanghai, a probationer of the China Inland Mission, designated to the province over which Bachelor was now superintendent! And in between was — GOD!

Bachelor was to escort the party of new workers from Shanghai to his province, and so I watched for an opportunity to ask for the story of that second 'losing'. One had to ask very gently, for one may not pry into the sacred inner chamber of another's heart, but I got a wonderful answer. Bachelor said simply, 'Y- (the land of his Lisu) was my Rachel, but K— (indicating the far place he was sent to) was my Leah'. His meaning was obvious. The Lisu were the love of his heart, but the other place had been even more fruitful to him in ministry. More fruitful than a HUNDRED-

FOLD? But 'He that loseth his life for My sake shall save it' — big savings *that*!

*   *   *

Then there is one more sketch of this inspiring life. The scene is back in Canada, outside a church, in a town not very far from the conference. The Conference Speaker that year was a famous evangelist from Wales, a wonderful exponent of the Victorious Christian Life, and he had just given a message in this little church before returning to the Old Country. He was standing on the sidewalk surrounded by men of the congregation, and as I passed by I heard one of them ask him, 'Doctor, what *is* a Spirit-filled life?'

Interested in such a vital question, eager to hear the distinguished visitor's answer, I slowed up and hung on the outskirts of the little group.

Doctor's sunny smile beamed on the questioner. 'I will answer,' he said, 'by an illustration. Two years ago I was first asked to be a speaker at The Firs Conference. The preceding year, a missionary from the China Inland Mission by the name of — (it was Bachelor!) had been at The Firs, and when I came the next year, the fragrance of his life *still rested* on everyone I met. THAT is a Spirit-filled life.'

The 'hundredfold'! 'No man who hath left . . . for My sake and the Gospel's . . . but shall receive an hundredfold.' A hundredfold in Lisuland, a hundredfold in America, back to China losing his life again, and more than a hundredfold among the Chinese!

'There is that maketh himself rich, yet hath nothing; there is that maketh himself poor, yet hath great riches.' (Prov. 13:7)

2

DOROTHY — ARE YOU WILLING FOR *THIS?*

THE YEAR BEFORE BACHELOR came to The Firs was my first summer conference. My coming had been prayed for by that incomparably dear and earnest pair — our Firs Conference 'Mother and Father'. Quite unconscious of the burden for me that had cost them so much prayer, I arrived, alone and rather shy, wondering what this thing 'a summer conference' would turn out to be. Just groping my way out of modern agnosticism, I was as molten wax — ready for any impression that might fall upon me; how often have I praised God that the 'impressions' that fell upon me at that time were so fully from Second-Mile lives.

I can still hear Conference Mother's cheery voice in her cry of joyous welcome, as I was introduced to 'our Edna' and told that I was to share with her a little cottage hidden in the woods some hundred yards away. But first there was a meeting about to start, would I just step into the living room for now (that same living room where the next year Bachelor was to tell us of his hun-dredfold) . . . The fire was sparkling in its place and a sea of young faces turned on me was slightly embarrassing, but their warm welcome soon made me feel entirely at home.

I would like to digress for a few pages in order to let you glimpse 'our Edna' and one other of that group on the floor. Of all these faces, only one stands out clearly in my memory — warm dark eyes and a beaming smile that of itself spoke of the kind loving heart that many recall with deep gratitude to God. 'Twin-Sister' she gaily labelled herself, because Conference Mother declared we looked alike, and I gladly accepted the compliment. Twin-Sister is a Vassar graduate, and Christian people tell you proudly that she comes from one of the richest families in her State, yet Christ has become to her the One who strips the seeming beauty from all other idols of the earth — riches, social position, and educational standing. She was dressed so simply and moved so sweetly and unaffectedly among the other young women of the Conference, that girls from very different backgrounds felt completely at home in her company, and no heart could shut up its confidences from that dear smile and sympathetic touch.

For years she wanted to join the rest of us as a missionary in China, but the delicate health of a widowed mother was quietly put first. At length God Himself opened the way, and added a fine husband for good measure. Conference Mother visited them in their home in China and wrote to me, 'Twin-Sister and her husband are a very definite spiritual force in C . . . and their home was a real centre for the Lord.'

'Our Edna' was leader of the young people's group that year, and we all treated her with the reverent gentleness which one naturally yields to a life with black crepe hung by its doorway, for Edna, still in her twenties, was newly widowed. She and her husband, Ellis, had been splendid young missionaries in one of China's largest cities, and had only been married a few months when they chose for their summer vacation a wooded spot where there was a swimming pool. They were both good swimmers, and just as they reached the edge of the pool one morning a cry for help rang through the air. They saw that a lady missionary who had gone in just before them was in danger. Without a pause Ellis leaped in after her, and shortly had her in safety, but strange to say he himself disappeared. Frantically the little bride plunged in after him, quite regardless of the wounds she was receiving as she was thrown against rocks, beaten and cut with plunging here and there in a desperate effort to sight her loved one. Long after hope of his life being saved must have gone, she kept on hunting and swimming and finally his body was seen washed up behind the falls. Gathering up the remainder of her strength Edna dived in again and returned, slowly dragging her precious burden to the bank.

Those who saw her said that when safe on shore with the beloved body, she just sank on a nearby log with her face buried in her hands. Lifting her eyes after a little while she saw a group of petrified Chinese watching her and the still tragic figure nearby. Forgetting her injuries and grief she got

up and ran to them, explaining that this was only
her dear Ellis's earthly tabernacle; the real part of
him, the soul that could never die, had gone to be
with Christ, and this hope is for every man. Do
you wonder we treated Edna with gentle rever-
ence?

It was my wonderful privilege to share Edna's
inner life during those conference days. She slept
with Ellis's Bible under her pillow; it was her last
thought at night and her first in the morning.
What lessons in practical Christian living I silently culled from that dear association! So it was
natural that, during Edna's last class with us,
when she called for lives to be dedicated to God's
service when or where He chose, I raised my hand
with the others. After living for ten days with Jesus
Christ revealed in a human life as He was in
Edna's, how could one help but yield? I was
surprised at her joy, surprised she did not expect
it.

> 'I saw a human life, ablaze with God,
> I felt a power Divine;
> As through an empty vessel of frail clay
> I saw God's glory shine!
> Then woke I from a dream,
> And cried aloud —
> "My Father, give to me
> The blessing of a life consumed by God,
> That I may live for Thee." '

I learned years afterwards the 'why' of Edna's
delighted joy. None of us happy young people
knew just how hard it was for Edna to 'lose' herself
and her new sorrow day after day, in finding and

giving us messages from His Word. But on that
last day she felt she was breaking. Before the class,
she ran into the room where the Conference Council were meeting, and cried, 'O I *can't* take them
today. Please one of you teach them! I haven't
anything to say, and it is the last meeting — *so*
important. *Please* let me out of this class!'

But Council knew well how Edna's life was
telling quietly on that happy young group, and
would not release her — just sent her back saying,
'We will pray for you all through that class'. And
God shone through the vessel of frail clay, and at
this moment there are five of us in China (not to
speak of those in other lands) testifying for Him,
who gave ourselves at that class which Edna felt
she 'couldn't take'.

*   *   *

Indwelt

'Not merely in the words you say,
Not only in your deeds confessed,
But in the most unconscious way
　　Is Christ expressed.

Is it a beatific smile,
A holy light upon your brow;
Oh no, I felt His Presence while
　　You laughed just now.

For me 'twas not the truth you taught
To you so clear, to me still dim
But when you came to me you brought
　　A sense of Him

And from your eyes He beckons me,
And from your heart His love is shed,
Till I lose sight of you and see
    The Christ instead.'

(by A. S. Wilson)

It was during the first few days of that Conference,
while my ideas of the Christian life were still in a
crude unmoulded state, that I remember seeing
Dorothy. She was brushing and fixing her wavy
brown hair before a mirror, and as often was the
case with this radiant young life, she was talking
merrily with others, the dimples playing in and
out of her pink cheeks with winsome sweetness. I
thought her very attractive and was so pleased
when she asked me to go for a walk with her.

Dorothy was secretly longing to 'speak just a
word for Jesus' with this young girl so obviously
still a question mark as far as the deeper things
went, and she had really that purpose in mind in
suggesting a walk. But somehow happy ridiculous
nothings would come to the surface and the whole
ramble was just one funny thing after another (I
remember a squashed toad on the pathway
sprang into symbolism as we attempted to discuss
the disciplines of life). When we parted Dorothy
felt she had been a failure, unconscious that the
one she had hoped to help was going away en-
chanted with this glimpse into the very human
sweetness of this Christ-like girl.

'. . . I felt His presence while
    You laughed just now.'

The Spirit-filled life cannot 'fail', it is fruitful

even when it may seem least to have done anything. That walk gave Dorothy 'influence' over
me when a 'sermon' would have created a permanent barrier. In fact at that time I carried a mental
suit of armour all ready to slip on quietly the
moment any 'old fogey' tried to 'preach' at me!

Oswald Chambers says, 'The people who
influence us most are not those who buttonhole us
and talk to us, but those who live their lives like the
stars in heaven and the lilies in the field, perfectly
simply and unaffectedly. Those are the lives that
mould us.' A great mistake is to think that a
Spirit-filled man or woman must always be casting sermons at people. Being 'filled with the Spirit' (which is a first qualification of Second Mile
People) is merely a refusing of self and a taking by
faith of the life of Christ as wrought in us by His
Holy Spirit.

'Many who claim by faith this fulness, and who,
up to the measure of their light, are yielded and
obedient, are disappointed and perplexed because
they are aware of no particular manifestation.
They expect a glowing sense of power . . . But let
us take to heart what others have pointed out, that
the Spirit's chief work is to make us HOLY. The
truest evidence is not gift but grace . . . The Spirit
will divide the gifts. One man may have a gift for
preaching, another a gift for intercession, another
a gift for personal dealing, and another by admi-
nistration. Still others may glorify their Lord by
some kind of seeming drudgery, even as lowly as
that of Brother Lawrence, who "practised the
presence of God" in the monks' kitchen.

"A work of lowly love to do
        For Him on Whom I wait."

'But let it be said again, once you open your
being to His fulness your life must be enriched;
you will never be the same again.'*

Dorothy threaded her way back through the
pine-scented air, and along the earth path in and
out among stately tall tree trunks. What was
wrong with her anyway? She had wanted to go for
that walk with Isobel to speak to her about her
soul, she had started out to do it, and then at the
end found she had not done it after all! There were
Edna and Twin-Sister, tactful soul winners both
. . . catch them doing such a trick, being such a
failure! But then they were clever — college
graduates, both of them — and Dorothy wasn't.
Was it cleverness that taught them to bring other
souls through to a decision for Christ? No.
Dorothy was too well taught seriously to believe
that — only the Holy Spirit can convict of sin, and
bring a soul through that mystery 'the second
birth'. Well then, was it that the Holy Spirit could
not use her, Dorothy? Discouragement and unbelief had gripped hands and for a moment she was
defeated.

Five hundred years before, a monk used to pace
the cloister of his monastery at Mount St Agnes,
and perhaps such thoughts assailed him. His was
a long and uneventful life, spent in copying manu-
scripts, reading and composing, and in the peace-
ful routine of monastic piety. Thomas à Kempis

* from A. S. Wilson's book, *Concerning Perplexities, Paradoxes
& Perils in the Spirit-led Path*

longed for nothing more than to be wholly his Lord's and used of Him, yet year after year passed and nothing spectacular or wonderful happened to him or through him. True, he was composing a book he meant to call the *Imitation of Christ*, but then it was hardly an original work at all. Only too well did he realize how much of it was merely culled from others' thoughts and clear vision, and how little was the simple product of his own mind. What he would not see was the beauty and depth of his own spiritual life, which runs throughout, weaving all foreign parts into one lovely mosaic, creating a book which has been for five hundred years the supreme call and guide to spiritual inspiration.

We fall in defeat when we try to 'judge' the work of the Holy Spirit in our lives; ours is to yield to Him in joyous faith, and not worry as to the kind or value of the fruit He is producing.

Dear Dorothy's special gift of the Spirit was her radiance, her shining happy joy in her walk with the Saviour, but I doubt if she ever knew she possessed it. She thought she should have been preaching, when as a matter of fact the Holy Spirit was using her gift of shining, to the very fullest extent in the life she had prayed to touch, and she need not have been so discouraged that afternoon. We must *take* the Spirit's fulness, as we take our salvation, by faith in God's promise that He is given to us.

A few days later, as we listened to a lecture, someone pointed to Dorothy and said, 'I suppose you know she is sailing for China, under the China

Inland Mission, in a few months' time?'

It came as a shock — for those days I was only beginning to think of yielding my own life for *home* service; foreign service had not yet loomed up on my mental horizon. I looked at the sweet earnest face — maybe she was not beautiful to others but she always was to me — the sparkling blue eyes, the pink cheeks where dimples loved to bask as in sunshine, the soft wavy brown hair. '*That* girl go bury herself in China! Why, what on earth *for*? She could easily get married and have a happy home in America; why waste all that sweetness on yellow old China?'

That old idea of mother's was in my mind too. Only old maids, misfits, folk who could not make good at home turned to the mission field . . . else *why* did they go? I was baffled and annoyed. I learned later that Dorothy *could* have 'married and stayed home'; what then was calling her away?

*   *   *

Conference ended, and everyone went back to the old routines of life, to apply the new vision to the old tasks. One day, a month or so later, in Port City, a phone call brought a happy sweet voice to my ear. 'I'm sailing tomorrow! Can't you run over and see me?'

Dorothy in Port City and only a few blocks away! What joy. 'Yes, I'll be there in five minutes — goodbye!' and out I ran, not waiting to change the clothes in which I had come from the schoolroom — for I was now a school teacher.

Dorothy was in the midst of last-minute packing, but soon cleared a place for me to sit, while she went on with her work, laughing and chattering and dimpling.

'Had some scare on the way here! We came by boat, and Mamma and I were just comfortably seated on deck, when suddenly Mamma said, "Dorothy! Have you got your ocean liner ticket which Mr Thompson (then secretary of the CIM in Port City) sent you?" We looked at each other blankly, the same thought in both our minds. If that ticket wasn't packed away in the bottom of a trunk which most likely was already in the bottom of the liner itself!

'"Oh Dorothy!" Mamma gasped, "All the money it cost — there will never be time to get hold of that trunk! What *will* we do?"

'I had Daily Light in my pocket, and took it out — I've often gotten help from it — and sure enough, there it was: "September 4th. Sit still, my daughter." You know the rest of that verse? — "until thou know how the matter will fall." Well it was just as if the Lord Himself had spoken to us, so we just took it from Him and refused to worry.

'When we got to Port City I had to face Mr Thomson and tell him, but' (here the dimples played enchantingly) 'he said it was not as bad as it looked, for he could get the ticket duplicated without much trouble. *Now doesn't it pay to trust the Lord?*'

And the blue eyes sparkled joyously up at me from the suitcase into which she was packing. She'd got in a 'preach' after all! But then her time had come; the Holy Spirit is never too early and never too late. It did not take her long to see I looked careworn.

'What's wrong, Isobel?' No dimples now, just sweet sympathy.

'Oh, it is the school teaching; I'm so unhappy, I feel such a misfit! All my life I've planned on teaching but now that I'm doing it I just seem to be a failure', and a long tale of the woes of early experiences in the schoolroom were poured into Dorothy's patient ears.

Finding it was nothing tragic the dimples returned — but carefully guarded — for Dorothy realized 'her time' had come, and she loved nothing better than to tell someone else about all her wonderful Lord had done for her. Leaving her packing she came and sat down beside me. I wish I could remember all she said, but Dorothy's preaching did not always stick in the memory — it was herself that was her most potent sermon.

> 'For me 'twas not the truth you taught
> To you so clear, to me still dim;
> But when you came to me you brought
> A sense of Him.'

I only know she told me stories out of her trials as a business girl, and how her Lord, as she continually looked to Him, unfolded new lessons of the Spirit-led life, the resting-in-Him life, the anxious-for-nothing life, the 'more abundant' life which is continual peace and frequent joy. Her dear laugh is forever associated now with Phil. 4:6 as she gave me 'her own' translation — 'Be anxious for nothing! — not even for your failures!'

I tried to learn, but the truth to her so clear, was to me still dim; it remained for Bachelor at the next year's Conference to teach me the practical 'how' of that life. From Dorothy I just drank in the inspiration of herself, the 'sense of Him', and the fact that this life of undisturbed peace was no mystic dream but a possible Reality who sat beside me with earnest sweet eyes, and soft pink cheeks.

I asked her for 'a verse' before we parted; Edna had given me 'My grace is sufficient for thee' (2 Cor 12:9). Dorothy, after a moment's thought said, 'This is my life verse, I will leave it with you. Col. 3:1: "If ye then be risen with Christ, seek those things which are above, where Christ sitteth on the right hand of God" ' . . . and her name is still written over that verse in my Bible.

At my request she also gave me a photo of herself, and all through that endlessly long teaching year it stood on my bureau, and during many an hour of doubt and trouble I would come and gaze at it, and somehow it helped.

> 'And from your eyes He beckons me,
> And from your heart His love is shed,
> Till I lose sight of you, and see
>   The Christ instead.'

*　　　*　　　*

Letters came after a while . . . happy Yangchow ones of studying the language, and trying to keep warm in the awful cold . . . an excited one telling of designations, Dorothy to far inland . . . a funny one filled with laughter over the ridiculous malad-

justments of Chinese road travel. Dorothy was
tall, five feet ten I think, and correspondingly
heavy, but she had to journey with a little girl who
had been a cabaret dancer before she was saved;
the two were to journey balanced on either side of
a mule litter, with the natural result that
Dorothy's side was always diving earthward,
while tiny Miss Dancer was always flying sky-
ward! It is surprising that they only had a real
upset once, but it was quite a serious one; however
the trials of that long month and a half's tedious
bumping, dust and hot sun were glanced over,
and always Dorothy's fountain of joy found something to laugh about.

By this time I had reached Moody Bible Institute, and there I found Dorothy was still lovingly
remembered. Satan does not shrug his shoulders
and bid you goodbye when you enter Bible Institute . . . the entrance is perfectly familiar to him,
and he has his own 'Master Key'. Trials and
temptations came in a flood upon the new student,
there was sometimes a desire to throw it all up, but
at such times the thought would come, 'Dorothy
has walked these halls, and went through many of
these same temptations; she did not run; if she
stuck to it, so can I,' and again I would go up to the
sweet picture-face on my bureau and sometimes
talk to it.

One of my greatest blessings while at Moody
was the group of wonderful young lives that God
gradually brought into mine; they are scattered all
over the world now . . . 'for His Name's sake' . . .
but they taught me more of practical Christian

living than classroom lectures. One of this dear number was the John of these pages. A quiet tenacity of spiritual purpose was what marked him out, and there was a thrill of joy when he told me he was accepted by the China Inland Mission. He sailed for the mission field while I had still a term's study to complete, and by the time I myself was ready to go, the door had closed.

Spring of 1927 found missionary work in China at a standstill. To John in the training home at Anking, and to Dorothy far inland, and to Bachelor who was then in Dorothy's province, came the order, 'evacuate!' An all-night wait at the river side with some ten men all in one tiny room, a crowded boat journey, and John was in Shanghai. But not so Dorothy and Bachelor.

Dorothy had found a nook in that far western province, with an older lady worker, older in the deep things of God as well as in years, and our young friend drank in joyfully all she had to teach; they were very happy. When ordered to flee they decided to sell all they had, rather than leave their things to be pillaged, and so in a short time they were ready to join the band of escaping missionaries. Travel overland, with anti-foreign feeling running so high and such dreadful deeds in Nanking still shuddering through one's memory, was out of the question. Bachelor was in charge of the group, and it was decided to flee by the Yellow River, on rafts of bloated skins.

There were several rafts needed, and peril and death tracked them. Robbers on shore, whirlpools that caught one of their rafts for several hours, and

then the tragic, grievous death of Dr King lifted
the smaller trials out of sight — the trials of
cramped space day after day in the tiny tent-like
shelter erected in the middle of the raft where they
slept, and the distressing lack of privacy. But
again all that discomfort was lightly touched upon
and a steadfast cheerfulness seems to drift across
the memory as one seeks to recall Dorothy's
account of those days.

On their arrival at Tientsin (the civilised
world) she had a joke on herself to relate. In those
far inland parts the woman missionary wears
Chinese costume, so when suddenly 'dumped out'
into such a stylish up-to-date city there was a
general consternation at the lack of appropriate
garments. Dorothy had retained a pretty satin
dress which she used to wear at home, and when
she heard the other ladies bewailing their plight
she hugged herself complacently at her own good
fortune — she had not only a foreign dress but a
lovely satin one! When, however, it was time to
'dress for dinner', Dorothy discovered to her immense chagrin that her treasured robe sat upon
her shoulders and refused to come down any
further — she had grown so plump that the dress
was now useless!

'Whatever did you do, Dorothy?'

With gales of laughter she replied, 'Made me a
dress out of my ponjee nightgown and wore that,
till better could be obtained.'

John, of course, was no stranger to the names of
Bachelor and Dorothy — he had loved to listen to
me tell of them in the old Moody days, and so

when he heard they had finally arrived in Shanghai, he was most eager to meet them. He was disappointed in neither. Bachelor's stories of Lisuland brought him what mine had not, a desire to give his own life to those dear people, but he said nothing to anyone. When, however, the 'uninformed' Shanghai Council designated him 'to tribes work in Y . . .' (the province where Lisuland is) he was sure that it was God's call, and sure also that many small leadings in another direction had now been crowned with all that was needed to complete the revelation of God's will. So one evening he electrified his unsuspecting comrades by the announcement of his engagement to Isobel!

Shortly after, during a social time among the 'evacuators', a tall young lady with roguish eyes and pink cheeks stood before him, and with proffered hand challenged a welcome — 'I-know-Isobel!' I do not know which enjoyed that meeting the more — each was enthusiastic about the other in recounting it all to the far-away waiting one.

It was natural, therefore, when John heard that Dorothy had been granted an early furlough for purposes of further Bible study, that he should come and ask if she would kindly take something to Isobel. Shyly he produced a modest little engagement ring — would she please be responsible for this reaching her friend?

WOULD she! How fast the dimples poked in and out of the pink cheeks! Of course she would be simply delighted at the opportunity. Inwardly she was thinking up a thousand ways to tease that same Isobel. Unfortunately for her mischievous

plans, she had to get off the boat before she came
to my home, and the treasure had to be entrusted
to an older missionary. I still remember the way
this lady looked me up and down and then said
significantly, 'You're a lucky girl!'

But Dorothy wasn't going to miss her chance to
'take a rise' out of her friend. In not many weeks
time I got word to prepare for a visit from her, and
that Twin-Sister would be coming with her. It was
with beating heart that I threaded my way to the
wharf that early morning — to see Dorothy was
excitement enough, but I was also going to meet
someone who had just lately seen and talked with
John! Sure enough as the crowd poured up the
gang plank there were the two beloved forms, and
soon I was in their arms. Twin-Sister, with that
sweet modesty and fine sense of feeling which
always marked her, immediately fell into the
background, and from there silently 'glowed' her
sympathy and joy, knowing full well how much
Dorothy and I had to talk over.

From the wharf to the quiet-nooked restaurant,
for breakfast, only laughing nothings were discussed. I was pronounced to 'look tired' and ordered
not to work hard. Dorothy herself was as young
looking, as pink cheeked and as radiant as the day
she left us four and a half years before, but decidedly plumper. 'Fatter!' she insisted disgusted-
ly, 'And oh, my family! You know I've a very
stylish young brother and sister at varsity! They
say I'm quite 'impossible' and are all on the
rampage to get me thinned to a willow line! No
chance of being the "fogey old mish" in my family'

— and so on, mischievously avoiding all topics that were so obviously languishing on the tip of my tongue. But when we finally got seated, Twin-Sister in the corner beside Dorothy and I opposite, when the little waitress had carried our order out, then Dorothy leaned across the table and with blue eyes roguishly fixed on me, and dimples tripping in and out, let loose her bomb, 'Well, Isobel, I *just love him!*' The naughty tease had so obviously planned it, was so obviously wishing to see if I would 'turn the other cheek also' that I couldn't help rising to the occasion, so eyeing her steadily back I said solemnly, 'So do I!' whereupon we all broke into happy laughter.

Joyous teasing sank frequently into earnest talk of deeper things, things touching the One Who stood as an invisible loving Presence over that small breakfast party — we did not have to mention *His* Name, it was graven so deeply, so dearly, on each of those three hearts that it was like a silent pervading perfume.

*   *   *

That summer conference lives in my memory in terms of Twin-Sister and Dorothy. I suppose we admire most in our friends those qualities in which we feel ourselves to be lacking. I, who was made to plunge and blunder, found a deep joy in watching Twin-Sister. There was a steadiness of spiritual gait about her that lifted her quite above other younger people of her age (neither she nor Dorothy was out of her twenties) and she had 'a

wise head set on young shoulders'. I never knew
her when that bright engaging smile was not *easily*
on top; I never knew her to preach a standard that
she herself did not live up to; there was not a
breath of the spiritual prig anywhere about her,
ever; and I never knew her to be in the slightest
influenced by that most insidious flattery — the
only too obvious adoration of the crowd. She was
idolized, and her company esteemed a high privilege, but she took it all with that good-natured
laugh of one whose eyes are fixed on something
quite different . . . fixed on Someone who had so
captured her heart that it would seem there was no
room in it any longer for love of things, or love of
self.

That year we lived in tents, and for every couple
of immature Christian girls there was placed one
who was older and deeper in the knowledge of
God. Dorothy was given the hardest two of all —
the kind of pert young rebels whom Christian
parents often send to a Summer Conference, fond-
ly hoping that they will 'come back different'!
Only a Dorothy could have influenced this smart,
pretty pair of teen-aged girls, and even Dorothy
had a hard time at first. They resented the obvious
reason for her presence in their tent, and were
even more alarmed to learn she was of that dread-
fully octopus-like species called 'missionary', so
they insisted on treating her as a kind of pious spy
come to discover and thwart all their best-laid
plans for dodging meetings and getting a good
time out of this pale thing — a Bible Conference!
On the surface they wore an elaborate politeness

towards her, but each gentle effort to get beneath
was met by a stiff backed, icy, 'Hands off!'
Dorothy, who was accustomed to warm atmos-
pheres of love, felt keenly the chilly air of her tent,
and more than once assured us that we had chosen
the wrong one to deal with that difficult pair. But
we just smiled . . . we knew what prayer and the
unaffected sweet joyousness of Dorothy herself
were bound to do. There was nothing of the pious
prude about our dear girl . . . she was so natural
and human in her Christian life, and so unconscious of possessing any power to influence others.

It was a wide-eyed surprise to that attractive
but naughty pair of young rebels, when some little
incident in the tent life brought forth ripples of
laughter and genuine enjoyment from their tall
'ogre'. Cautiously they began to test her out . . .
was this part of her 'game', or was she really as
simple and as lovely as she seemed? And at every
test she rang true. To those alert young things who
had firmly and resolutely closed their pretty ears
to every message or word about the Christ, came
that subtlest of wooings . . . the Master's own
winsome life lived out in human form, lived naturally, sweetly, abundantly. They suspected deep
astute traps to 'catch' them, they quite believed if
it were possible they would be dragged, as it were,
by the scruff of the neck, to the feet of the Lord —
what they never expected was this life of inexplic-
able beauty which enthralled without making any
attempt to do so.

I do not know their after career, but I do know
that before Conference ended each had given

Dorothy some token of that enthralling, and the
tent atmosphere which began as veiled warfare
ended in warmest fellowship.

Autumn again brought a parting of our ways;
Twin-Sister returned to home duties; Dorothy left
for Biola for further study; I, at last, sailed for
China.

*   *   *

Spring of 1929. Yangchow, with its blessed restful
days and interesting new studies and friendships,
was over, and our party had arrived in Shanghai
en route to its inland designation. A casual remark, 'Do you know Dorothy B. . . is here? Just
got off the boat,' sent me pelting along verandas,
upstairs and bursting into the bedroom which I
was told she was sharing with her beloved fellow
worker. What a joyous cry of welcome! How
proudly and roguishly Dorothy turned herself
around and challenged my congratulations —
'I've lost 30 lbs!' Then the introduction to Fellow
Worker of whom I had heard so much and whose
quiet thoughtful maturity was a splendid background to Dorothy's radiant youthfulness. A
Lisuland scene has sometimes recalled them. Our
Lisuland is rock but scattered about, embedded in
the surface soil, are multitudinous smaller rocks.
These have the mellowed appearance of age and
experience, for every year the blazing heat of
forest fires scorches them black, and then the
fierce mountain wind comes and blows them clean
and cool again. In the springtime, lovely purple

violets appear at the edge of these stones, their
white slender roots slipping down and under,
almost into the gray granite, and their soft frag-
rant heads lifted against its protecting solidity.

Gray rock and sweet violet were these two.
Fellow Worker was the embedded rock which had
gone through the fire and bitter blast of missionary life lived in the midst of heathendom, and
Dorothy was the gentle flower whose roots clung
affectionately to the firm strength of her experienced comrade.

Of those Shanghai days two pictures of Dorothy
plead for admittance. One is chancing upon her
and Fellow Worker one early morning before
breakfast as they paced up and down the compound walk, talking together in low tones. As I
approached, Dorothy cried out, 'I am being
scolded for not having my packing done by the
hour ordered. You see,' casting a loving glance at
Fellow Worker which showed the 'scold' must
have been a very kind one, 'She is my "Mamma"
as well as my partner, and thinks and orders for
me . . . *and expects obedience!*' with a mischievous
glance. Dorothy had often told me that this
'Mamma-Partner' had also been a richly deep
Bible teacher to her, and the loving relationship
which existed between them was beautiful to see.

The second picture is Dorothy on the train that
took her far inland. I was down to see her off,
because she was 'Dorothy' but also because she
was taking some new workers — my fellow Yang-
chow-ites — in with her. At that station trains
were invariably off schedule and overcrowded,

because they sold more tickets than they had seats. Therefore to get a compartment you must go early and grab places for yourself and party, for your boxes and suitcases and whatnot. The 'grabbing' often involves diving and dodging, knocking heads, bumping, with eddies of dust filling throat and soiling person, and it can be trying, but with Dorothy it was only an excuse for letting loose that merry tongue. Soon she had the party in an uproar of laughter and at my last sight of her she was saying, 'Here! Here! this won't do at all! New workers to take their seniors so lightly! I must teach them to respect the dignity of their elders,' and she was trying to straighten out those uncontrollable dimples and assume a mien of sanctimonious gravity when the train pulled out.

*   *   *

Three or four months later and many hundreds of miles distant, in a busy little market town on a busy mountain-girt plain, I and my fellow worker were just settling down for what we hoped would be some months of intensive work. One evening, the door of our sitting room was suddenly darkened by a tall, quick-moving form — our senior missionary, to whom we had just said goodbye in the provincial capital city nine days previously, not expecting to see him again for many another month. He spoke with suppressed excitement, waving our exclamations into silence. 'I've come to get you two, and take you back to the capital! The governor's army is away fighting the neighbour province and a huge band of brigands have seized this moment to attack us. They are marching on their way to attack the capital now and it is believed you are right in their path . . . we must be off by dawn tomorrow and race them to the city. God grant we get there first!'

Pushing us into seats, he himself sat down and continued, 'That isn't all. Yesterday the arsenal exploded, destroying a large part of the city; our house was badly shaken, some windows smashed and the roof cracked, but the other CIM compound was quite wrecked. . . . No, no lives were lost, praise God.'

It was not till we were seated for a cup of tea that he remembered a third piece of news. 'Oh yes, there is something else; I am afraid it is bad news for you, sister', turning sympathetically to me. 'News has come that Dorothy B. . . is dead . . . died of typhus fever; there has been a lot of it there following the famine, you know.'

The words dropped on my consciousness with a thud that 'brigands' and 'arsenal explosion' had failed to effect.

'Dead . . . my Dorothy DEAD' . . . the sitting room and its inmates faded out of sight and I seemed to be left in space with the great big terrible letters D-E-A-D written across the darkness. 'My bonny Dorothy . . . those pink dimpled cheeks . . . that radiant young life . . . gone? Oh no!' Rebellion hot and insistent rose within; it was surely a mistake, perhaps it was someone else; blinded with tears I looked up to say so, but the kindly pitying eyes of my senior missionary told all too plainly there was no mistake. 'But I just saw her a few months ago, said goodbye to a laughing bonny girl with years of splendid life ahead'! . . . Dead.

The pain of that evening reaches out over the years to me and grips afresh. It does not seem possible (when it is *your* loved one it happens to!) that so much radiant young life can be laid cold in a few feet of earth and covered over with soil. Oh *no*! That is not the end, blessed be God!

'He that doeth the will of God *abideth forever*.' And where that bright spirit is now, I am persuaded I will be someday also, for did we not have the same faith, live the same life, His life? If heaven held no Christ, it must still be heaven because of the Dorothys there, because of those marvellous ones who have gone on before us; surely having lived the same, fought for the same, believed the same they must also share the same? What a wonderful heritage of friends is waiting for us over yonder! And yet to each of us, One Face must outshine all the others, a Face the love-light of which is past the brightness of the sun, and does away with need of candle or burning planet.

'And His servants shall serve Him, and they shall *see His Face*' . . . it is our promise, our hope, our heaven.

In the midst of her grief, Fellow Worker whose life, so to speak, had merely brushed close to mine in passing, she who turned from the new grave to the house with its empty chair and room, she remembered the love I had for Dorothy, and wrote a dear long letter of those last days. She had faithfully nursed her, and often had their conversation turned on the way of the Cross. 'Of all plans of ensuring success,' said Thomas Ragland, years before in India, 'the most certain is Christ's own — that of becoming a corn of wheat, falling into the ground and dying.' As Dorothy's last hours were approaching she seemed to know it, and her eyes called the tender nurse to bend over and listen. 'Are you willing for *this*?' she whispered.

It was her last word, but its searching question has echoed and re-echoed in my heart. It comes whispering down over these intervening years . . . 'Except a corn of wheat fall into the ground and die, it abideth alone; but IF IT DIE, it bringeth forth much fruit' (Jn. 12:24) What if the corn of wheat be young and lovely? . . . What if it be a *literal dying*? . . . 'Are you willing for *this*?'

Said Earth's loveliest and strongest of all her manhood, in the flower of His youth, 'The cup which My Father hath given Me, shall I not drink it?' . . . and they 'led Him away to crucify Him.'

'Captain beloved, battle wounds were Thine,
Let me not wonder if some hurt be mine;
Rather, O Lord, let my deep wonder be
That I may share a battle wound with Thee.

O golden joy that Thou, Lord, givest them
Who follow Thee to far Jerusalem;
O joy immortal, when the trumpets sound,
And all the world is hushed to see Thee
                                        crowned.'
                              (Amy Carmichael)

3

BUD — THE INDEFATIGABLE
SOUL WINNER

IT WAS DINNER TIME around the table of a China
Inland Mission Home in Canada, where I was
spending five weeks as a candidate. The conversation happened upon the young missionaries of the
previous summer who had been in the Home in
their turn, most of whom had been my fellow
students at Moody; but one boy, who had sailed in
John's party, was a stranger, and the description
of him caught my imagination.

'He is an indefatigable soul winner,' said the
hostess. 'I will never forget going down to the train
to see them off for the western coast. He did not
travel with the rest of that party but by himself,
and he would not get into his own coach but hung
on the platform till the train was about to pull out.
Then I knew why! On the end was a car crowded
with men going to work in the harvest fields of the
prairies, and he jumped into their coach, forgoing
the roomy comforts of his own, in order to do
personal work among them. An indefatigable soul
winner — that's what he is.'

*　　　*　　　*

When John's letters began to arrive at my door,
'Bud' figured in many. He had a grand contempt
for compromise, or diluting the Word of God with
'but's and 'however's.

> 'From subtle love of softening things,
> From easy choices, weakenings,
> O Lamb of God, deliver me!'

might have been written of Bud.

He was very business-like in his Christian life.
He had previously been a telegraph operator for
one of our great Canadian railways; when he
received an instruction over the wire, it was his
custom to accept it implicitly for just what it said;
and the instructions were not always attractive —
sometimes they ordered him to far lonely and
distant outposts. When he received one like this,
he did not greet it in the dubious manner with
which many modern Christians approach God's
Book of Instructions. He did not eye it all over,
then say to himself, 'Now I wonder if this really
did come from the Boss! Just as likely as not it is a
forgery by his secretary . . . though why, I cannot
for the life of me think! But I had better be very
careful about this and investigate it thoroughly
before proceeding to obey.'

Nor did he receive it in a second favourite
attitude — 'It doubtless *is* from the Boss . . .
sounds like him . . . but how very drastic! Sending
a young single inexperienced fellow like me to *that*
kind of a place. It must be he did not quite mean
what he says. Now let me see, just how could we
interpret this to make it more plausible?'

Nor did he adopt a third even more popular

plan — 'Oh dear! This looks rather disagreeable; guess I'd better not read it very carefully . . . it is just as well to be a little ignorant . . . one can always say then, that one did not understand.'

He simply took it at face value — and *went*; and incidentally some small western Ontario towns owe a new spiritual blessing and revival in their little churches to Bud because he did not question, but just went.

Near to one home we had in China was a big fascinating water-mill. A bright little creek tumbling down an embankment had been captured and turned into usefulness; as its waters made the small descent they were caught by and made to turn a big wooden wheel, which in turn was attached to a huge stone wheel on the floor above which revolved in a narrow groove where the rice to be ground was placed. That massive stone was made to roll simply by the pressure of the brook upon the water wheel, not at all by the fact that there was, or was not, any grain to grind! We more than once peeked into the floury interior and watched that big imposing stone come rolling along at a great rate, but over an empty trough, wearing itself out and accomplishing nothing! Some Christians are like that stone wheel. They are moved by the pressure of public opinion, which expects some amount of 'church activity' from a church member, and so they go round and round, often a dignified and interesting spectacle, but grinding nothing, wearing themselves thin and nothing to show for it.

Bud never wasted his strength to grind air, but he never begrudged it, either, if there was real grain in the trough. At the Training Home in Anking there was the usual six-hour-a-day schedule of study to go through, which very often leaves one fatigued and unable to bring the usual freshness to prayer and Bible study. Whenever Bud felt this spiritual barrenness about to clutch, he would forego his dinner and take that extra time for nourishing his inner life. The 'mother' at that home is famous for her delicious cooking, and undoubtedly tempting odours and the happy buzz of voices in glad fellowship would drift up to him, but they did not lure him away. He would stay with his Lord until that inner thirst was quenched, and preferred to feed his spirit rather than his body. If it increased or bettered the Boss's business, what did a meal now and then signify? It does not in the money world — why be more lustful of physical comforts in the spiritual realm?

Another individual trait in this singular boy was his intrepid insistence on getting the most out of his investment — the life he had given over to Jesus Christ. Again his business-like attitude is exhibited. He was determined to know how others, who were notably successful spiritually, planned their lives and habits. On arriving in Shanghai he inquired who were the outstanding Christian leaders, and on learning their names and addresses took himself off to look them up. It made no difference that he was a nobody and they were prominent and busy men, he introduced himself and his questions, and I do not think he ever met with rebuff . . . but he no doubt learned a great deal.

Said Dr Goulburn, 'The greatest saints who ever lived, whether under the Old or New Dispensation, are on a level which is quite within our reach. The same forces of the spiritual world which were at their command, and the exertion of which made them such spiritual heroes, are open to us also.' If one can be a great spiritual force, a great channel of blessing to mankind, or a nobody, merely by one's choice, why not choose to get and give the most out of life? Especially as one has only *one* life to invest.

Shanghai evacuation days brought a delightful opportunity to the keen soul winner. The streets teemed and thronged not only with the usual motley of Chinese, Indians and Japanese, but with foreign soldiers and sailors of several nations. The forces of evil were working 'in season and out of season' to entrap these easy victims, and no one who loved God and His kingdom could stand by in idleness. Spare hours often saw Bud slipping out of the door with his pockets bulging with tracts, to be distributed with eager loving word to the men he encountered; and evenings would find him at some gathering place where the souls of men were loved and won.

A strong friendship was growing up between John and this fellow missionary whom he admired so much, and at last one day, a snapshot of the two of them arrived in Canada. I could hardly wait to examine it, and after one long look I laughed outright, 'So *that* is "Bud"! Well, who ever would have thought it!'

I wonder how you picture an 'indefatigable soul-winner', a 'man of prayer'? Short, stalky, grim, serious-faced with burning eyes? Well this snapshot revealed a tall slim debonair youth, decidedly good looking with dimples, real dimples, in his cheeks. 'A man of prayer' . . . with dimples! How God loves to surprise us; how often life is not as we picture it.

*   *   *

Bud and John were designated to neighbouring provinces. Several years later, after John and I were married, Bud had to come all the way to our provincial capital in order to get suitable glasses. Meanwhile, a little drama was being enacted in a busy Chinese town, a day south of the capital. I was sitting on the very narrow upper ledge we liked to style the 'veranda', with the whole changing panorama of Chinese life right under my feet, so to speak, when I saw John coming down the street with the mail. His manner betokened excitement. . . upstairs he dashed two at a time and burst in on me waving a Shanghai letter, 'What do you know! We're appointed to go *west*, to start right away, WEST, think of it!' West had always been spelt in golden letter to both of us.

After a jig of joy (behind closed doors) we settled down to read details. We were to make our home at an old centre of the mission's and the

purpose was twofold. First, members of The Two
Hundred, designated to forward movement work
in the west, were to live with us till they got on
their linguistic feet (and so be saved the trials of
housekeeping without the language) and second-
ly, John was to scout around those vast unworked
districts, preaching, but also hunting for suitable
centres, suitable houses for the young people
eventually to occupy. And we were to start at
once!

'A new vision for a new task.' How often has the
Lord had to stop this eager pair, and give us just
that. Arrival at the capital city revealed the bald
fact that horses and coolies to go west, or anywhere else, were not to be had . . . the Military
were busy, and had commandeered all that were
available.

Another pair of newly weds were also held up in
the same city. I wonder if you noticed, that in
quoting Mk 10:29, 30 Bachelor left out a word or
so?* The verse says if any man has left house,
lands etc and 'wife and children'! Well, the time
had come for the Lord to give him his hundredfold
in that respect too, not a harem of wives but quite
really 'one in a hundred'. Her spirituality united
to unusual charm had finally given Bachelor a
happy marriage. Two beautiful baby girls came
gradually in after years, and now Bachelor no
longer has that wistful look in his eyes which I
remember seeing at Conference one day, when a
sweet little girl ran past him and he put out his
hand and caught her close and drew her onto his
* See page 20

knee. His 'hundredfold' would seem to be complete.

It was a breathtaking moment when John learned that Bud had arrived in the same city! But not until after the Chinese prayer meeting that Saturday evening did I at last meet him face to face. It was a happy occasion, for one sometimes learns to love these Second-Mile People long before it is granted to meet them in the flesh, and Bud's spiritual fire and earnestness had been a blessing to me. But the greater joy was when the two men friends clasped hands, and it was not surprising when, one evening soon after, John burst into our bedroom with the words, 'Isobel! Bud wants me to spend the night with him in prayer — you don't mind, do you?' And soon he was running over to the chapel, eager for that fellowship which binds closer than any other.

It was a sadder and a wiser man that returned the morrow morn. I knew something had happened the moment I saw his face, and when the door was closed we sat down to 'share'.

'Well — Bud just broke me all up last night, dear', he began slowly and obviously with difficulty. 'After we had prayer for a while, Bud told me he had something to tell me, and it was that he was very disappointed in me — especially after hearing me preach in Chinese Saturday night.'

'Disappointed in you!' His bride was all sticking out with porcupine quills.

'Yes dear, now don't get excited, for he is *quite right*. He said that after the spiritual times we had had in Shanghai he had expected a lot of me, and

he feels the Lord expects it too. And then in my
message Saturday — well that earnest fire-for-
Christ just wasn't there, and he was so disappointed he could not help but tell me, though it
cost him a lot to do so.

'You see, Bud is not like other people. He views
things from a different angle. Most other missionaries would have complimented me on my
clear Chinese . . . you know how they do lately,
and' — here John hung his head — 'to tell the
truth I noticed Bud did not say a word about it and
I guess . . . I guess I was rather looking for him to
do so. Anyway,' the head came up with a jerk, a
determined jerk, 'I know he is right, and I am sure
that a spirit of loving earnestness and care for the
souls of men might have done something more
than was done that night. But I guess I had
gradually got to like to hear people talk about my
good Chinese, and unconsciously I was thinking
more of my idiom than I was of the souls of the
men before me. Anyway I know Bud was right,
and there in the chapel I broke down and cried
and asked to the Lord to forgive me . . . and I
believe He has. . . .I think, Isobel, it would do you
good to have a time of prayer, too?'

So together we knelt down and asked the Christ
whom our souls loved, not to let *anything* blur our
vision of His Cross, and its message to China.

'From all that dims Thy Calvary,
        O Lamb of God, deliver me.'

How unexpected and subtle are the temptations on the foreign field! How many a missionary
has dulled the fine edge of spiritual earnestness by

an ambition to become an accomplished Chinese speaker; not that that ambition is wrong — for how can one 'adorn the doctrine of God' if he does not give heed to the necessary vehicle of his speech? — but it is fraught with danger.

On the same boat that brought me (and six or seven others) to China, was Miss Ruth Paxson. She was tired from many meetings and needed a rest, yet at the sight of that eager little group of going-to-be-missionaries, she was touched, and consented to give us an hour a day. She spoke on 'life on the highest plane' and touched intimately upon missionary temptations and problems. I remember so well the slow emphasis and earnest look with which she said, 'You are not all going to get the language equally well.' In the silence that followed it was as if a blank wall slit open for a moment, and threw into view vistas of unconceived experiences.

One usually comes to the foreign field with one thing in mind — winning the Chinese for Christ. Happy the one who has had deeper knowledge, and comes just focussed on Christ Himself; not on service, not on soul winning, just on the Lord, our Life. The first thing that meets you is 'the language', and it invariably has favourites. One, perhaps, gets it quickly, becomes elated and plunges in to try and break the record made by the previous Brilliant One; another, who was quite as clever at home, is unconsciously piqued, and strains to keep up; still a third finds herself slow, and before she knows it, is working overtime, endangering health and peace of heart, to try and hide the prickly fact. There is a subtle tendency for the focus, which is on Him, gradually and unwittingly to swing a little off until it is pointing on to Chinese Study, not on to Christ alone. A sly whisper sometimes comes, to offset that peculiar 'disturbed' feeling, 'After all it is for Him. The sooner you can get the language well the sooner you can win souls' and often the result is 'While Thy servant was busy here and there . . . He was gone.'

It need not be so, but how many times it seems that between the hour of landing in China, and the hour when full-time evangelistic work is begun, 'something' gets lost! After a year or so one is at last able to speak! . . . and finds he has nothing to say. One came to China rich; 'Quiet Times' were alive, luxuriant with the unveilings of truths from His word. Then, the language acquired, one goes to draw on the old fount, and it is dried up, or worse still, one is unconscious that the previous power has left.

I wish to digress a moment to show the 'cure' for this, by a picture.

Among the members of The Two Hundred who later came to live with us was one young man we call our 'Saint'. For pure goodness and real humility none of us can touch him. Although a college graduate (which he would never tell you) he rates himself, simply, as nothing — and there are people who see no further and accept him at his own rating . . . but being a saint, he does not resent it.

'Blessed are the single-hearted, for they shall have an abundance of peace' said the old monk of 'uneventful' life, and Saint, single-hearted unto God, carries about with him an atmosphere of unruffled peace. Single-hearted from the start, his 'focus' never swerved a point.

The 'picture' is one John drew for me, and it has often blessed me in this language problem. One afternoon John had occasion to go into Saint's room and found him, not at his Chinese studies like everybody else at that hour, but seated with his open Bible in front of him, meditating. He rose and greeted John quietly and courteously, and seemed quite oblivious that, to his senior missionary, his occupation was unexpected.

'I think that is Saint's secret,' John said in recounting it later, 'he *takes time* to feed on the Word.' The only safe way to avoid pitfalls at home or in China, is to keep close to the Source *independent of other's actions or opinions*.

It is notable, we think, that during this can't-speak-the-language period, Saint was instrumental in a Chinese man coming to the Lord Jesus.

*   *   *

The next Friday afternoon, Bud was chosen to be the speaker at our usual weekly China Inland Mission prayer meeting. I do not remember much that he said, but we can never forget the results. He finished by saying he felt sure God had not brought so many of us together at that time (for gradually more and more missionaries had got 'shut in' with us) without a purpose, and surely

He longed to pour out upon us special blessing, if
we would only take time to wait upon Him for it
. . . did anyone else have this same feeling?

Mrs Bachelor immediately spoke up, and in her
sweet way voiced a desire for just this very thing.
She was followed by John, while I sat, feeling as if
all within was scorching fire; I knew perfectly well
that if anyone needed a fresh quickening it was
me.

That field was, at that time, much hampered by
disunion among its missionaries. There was a
surface courtesy but no real love, such as the
Christ commands us to have. 'This is My com-
mandment,' He said, in those sacred last hours,
'that ye love one another, AS I HAVE LOVED
YOU.' Outspoken criticism did not heal matters,
and if you agreed with one circle, it naturally
followed that you did not have much fellowship
with the other. And in this matter of 'talking' I had
been guilty, too.

I was really without excuse, for I had been
carefully warned against this very thing, before I
ever sailed for China. However by 'gossip' I had
imagined was meant the passing on of puny tittle-
tattle, and to resist was more or less prepared; but
Satan is a wily foe who does not attack the place
that is being guarded; so when it assumed the form
of 'discussion' of a certain course of action, or a
certain method of work, it seemed but natural to
fall in line.

Later, Bachelor explained the biblical position
on this question — 'If thy brother trespass . . . go
and tell him his fault BETWEEN THEE AND

HIM ALONE' (Matt. 18:15). Bachelor himself never fell into this trap. When he thought he saw me being entangled he had taken me aside and urged me to refuse to listen when others wanted to 'talk'. But those others were senior missionaries and it seemed a costly thing to do — it had obviously cost Bachelor his popularity with each group, for his quiet strongly-visible disapproval, and his absolute refusal to listen to criticism when the person discussed was not present, aroused keen resentment, and he was disliked as a result. I had been too weak to pay that price, yet I always knew that the party I sided with did not like me in spite of my compromise, and so I really gained nothing in friendship, and on the other hand lost out terribly in another direction, for I had seemed to 'turn sour' spiritually.

Bud's message that afternoon, and the earnest desire for more holiness expressed by people like Mrs Bachelor who could not have had any scorching fire within such as I had, were too much, and in a flood of tears I tried to make my confession.

Others also were touched, and confessions and longings were poured forth. Bachelor, whose heart had been nearly broken over the condition he knew existed, was delighted beyond words, and was not slow to reach out after what the Lord was so clearly offering.

As superintendent he ordered all work that could possibly be laid aside, to stop, and the missionaries were invited to give their time to prayer for revival. No period was 'set', for who knew how long the Holy Spirit needed to search us? But it turned out to be about ten days; each day we spent from early morning till noon before the Lord, and again met together in the evenings.

Bud was in his element, and was a blessing to older people, even to Bachelor himself. Sins were confessed and forgiven, and a new spirit of affection in the Lord was manifest. Bachelor was anxious to see that under-the-surface feud wiped out, and Bud was anxious to see the missionaries burdened to pray for revival, so these two subjects were constantly brought before us, and God answered prayer.

When finally, coolies were obtainable and we scattered to all points of the compass, a real and definite work of the Spirit of God had been accomplished.

*   *   *

We have never seen 'the indefatigable soul-winner' since, and as neither he nor John took letter writing seriously we know little of the details of his after life. But that it was poured forth for Christ, there is no doubt.

Conditions in his own province were much similar, missionaries given to criticising one another's methods, and the Chinese churches 'dead'. (By the way, after our prayer meetings ended, a similar series had been carried on among the Chinese church members, with somewhat similar results.) Bud went back with definite purpose of praying down revival in that district also.

We had all been stirred by having our attention called to the place prayer has had in all the famous revivals, and in fact in the lives of those men who have meant most to Christ's church.

Hudson Taylor said: 'The sun has never risen upon China without finding me at prayer'; in our province, in the summer time, it is light enough at four-thirty in the morning to read one's Bible.

Bishop Andrews . . . spent five hours every day in prayer and devotion.

'John Welsh . . . thought the day ill spent which did not witness eight or ten hours of closest communion..'*

The saintly Fletcher spent a whole night once a week in the presence of his Lord.

Christmas Evans continually gave long periods to prayer; in his diary he says of one occasion, 'I waited three hours before God, broken with sorrow . . . on the following day I preached with such new power . . . that a revival broke out that day and spread through all Wales.'

Matthew Henry, whose Commentary is still a treasure house for students of the Bible, arose regularly at four a.m. for purposes of devotion and meditation; and so one could go on.

To this matter of prayer, Bud applied all the strength of that 'out-for-business' quality, which marks him.

'Jesus Christ demands of the man who trusts Him the same reckless sporting spirit that the natural man exhibits. If a man is going to do anything worthwhile, there are times when he has

* Meyer

to risk everything on his leap, and in the spiritual domain Jesus Christ demands that you risk everything you hold by common sense and leap into what He says, and immediately you do, you find that what He says fits on as solidly as common sense.'*

But to pray as the men abovementioned did, means sacrifice.

'Notice,' wrote Dr Taylor to his wife 'in Cor. I: 18, the connection of the Cross with power. Do not many lives lack power because they do not love the Cross?'

Bud was bound that he was not going to 'lack power' because his flesh shrank from the sufferings of the Cross.

In a year or so's time (notice it was not in a day) we heard of special quickening among the missionaries in his province and of a similar intensive prayer session for revival; Bud brought his bride to it to pass their honeymoon in this ministry. It was not long afterwards that Bud had a 'breakdown' — brain fag it was named — and they returned to Canada.

Last year we received a circular letter from someone in Bud's province, telling of deeper revival spreading from missionaries to the hitherto 'dead' Chinese churches.

China calls rumour a 'wind sound'. Can you not feel that these 'wind sounds' have a very definite voice running through them . . . the voice of a man praying, hour after hour, day after day . . . praying for the revival of God's work?

*   Oswald Chambers

He had 'risked everything on his leap'; what if it did mean an exhausted brain? An early furlough home?

'Then took Mary a pound of ointment of spikenard, very costly, and anointed the feet of Jesus, and wiped His feet with her hair; and the house was filled with the odour of the ointment' (John 12:3).

'But when His disciiples saw it, they had indignation saying, "To what purpose is this waste?"' (Matt. 26:8)

'Then said Jesus, "Let her alone; she hath wrought a good work."'

Bud has taken the costly spikenard of his life and his young manhood, and recklessly poured it out at Christ's feet. Dare you and I stand aside and call it 'waste'? Christ did not. He *accepted it*, and gave a loving commendation. You and I may not criticise where Christ commends.

*   *   *

Bud once told us this story, in answer to a question as to what method of preaching he preferred. He said that he usually gave just the message of the life and resurrection of our Lord, for he felt that to one who had no Christian background, this was the most potent introduction.

'I have had wonderful experiences in giving that story,' he said. 'Once I was walking along the road, and I was tired. I sometimes have spells of awful nausea and faintness come over me' (I learned later from his wife that his digestion was nearly ruined by eating poorly prepared food made by an incompetent cook-boy in his bachelor days) 'and on this occasion, one of these spells overtook me. I felt I was going to go unconscious if I did not sit down, but the only thing in sight was a stone by the side of the road, so I sank on to it. A Buddhist nun, attracted I guess by the sight of a foreign man alone and obviously ill, came up and stood and looked at me. I felt I should preach to her but was so sick and nauseated that for a moment I faltered. However I started on my usual text, the story of Christ, and do you know that by the time I had finished, all the illness had left me and I felt as if I had a new fresh body? I can never forget the physical exhilaration that the Lord gave to me at that time, and though I never saw her again, I believe that nun will be saved — she seemed so deeply impressed.'

He told me this sweet little 'second mile' tale, perfectly unconscious of the picture of the indefatigable soul winner he was drawing; he was simply thrilled with the healing power of the mere story of Calvary. But the revelation of the selflessness of Christ's servant, striving to preach through physical nausea and illness, never left us. It brings to mind the form of Another, who weary and tired, sat Himself upon a well to rest. But when a woman, a needy one, chanced by, He forgot self in longing after her soul, and He too, preached up through the exhaustion which was laying Him low, and reached out for her salvation. And He also, found a new strength come into the tired body — a strength so fresh, so sweet, that when food was finally put before Him, He had lost desire for it, and gently said, 'My meat is to do the will of Him that sent Me, and to finish His work.'

Do you not think that as Christ in heaven looked down upon that tired sick missionary-child of His trying to push his spirit up through the weight of the physical that chained and bound it down — do you not think as Christ poured into that spent form an 'exhilaration', a new fresh strength, that He remembered His own time of need, there by the well of Sychar? 'My grace is enough for you, for my strength FULLY UNDERSTANDS in your weakness' (as a Dohnavur schoolboy once translated 2 Cor. 12:9).

How loving is that 'fully understands', how restful just to lie back upon it and receive the freshness, the 'exhilaration'!

4

JENNY — A NOBODY

'FOR VERILY, BY LOVING myself amiss, I lost myself, and by seeking and sincerely loving Thee alone I found myself and Thee, and then through love have brought myself to yet deeper nothingness' (Thomas à Kempis).

Jenny is not her real name. I call her this because of a quaintly funny 'family anecdote' which is too interesting to miss.

Jenny is tenth of a big Scotch family of fourteen, and by the time she arrived babies had ceased to be thrilling or perhaps very much desired. At any rate they were not spoiled with petting, but on the contrary thought their own little thoughts, dreamed their own little dreams, and planned their own little plans more or less unnoticed.

Our little friend was born with clever fingers; no matter what the work is, from kneading bread to writing intricate Chinese characters, she excels over most of the common herd. When she was just a little girl at school, one afternoon the teacher was giving a drawing lesson and gave the unusual order: 'Draw from your imagination!' Jenny was in her element and the small careful fingers set to work eagerly; in what seemed but a little time she was startled to hear her teacher's voice over her shoulder say, 'Why child! You are a genius!'

Thrilled through and through, for she was not accustomed to being picked out of the crowd like that and praised, the little one flew home to share her good news. With pink cheeks of joy and excitement she told the wonderful news in the bosom of that large family.

'Ho! Ho! Ho!' laughed a big brother, seeing a grand chance to show off that mother wit which rarely received its due attention in this big crowd. 'Called you a genius, did she? Say, what's wrong with your ears, young one? *You* a genius! Go on, she said you were a *jenny-ass*!' and tickled to pieces with his remarkable pun he never saw the light go out of the small face, nor knew that a lovely dream castle had tumbled down into brown earth at his rough touch.

Just a jenny-ass! Why of course, that must have been what teacher said; how foolish to dream that *she* might ever do anything rather better than her fellows? The sensitive little thing fell back out of sight, and the older ones chattered on, not conscious that a child's heart had been wounded, and that the joke of that evening was going to leave a scar for many years to come.

All through the years of growth into womanhood, the thrill of that genius-dream which in the careless hands of the uncomprehending had crumbled into grey dust, was never forgotten, and an echo of that child's disappointment rang dimly in my ears on receiving a letter from her the other day. I had feared that a certain alluring temptation might assail her, but her reaction showed the bitterness of the past had become the safeguard of the future. No need to fear, she wrote, that temptation was for the well-educated, for those who might actually expect the limelight. And then she added these words, 'and what am I? A nobody.'

So this little nobody of a big Scotch family early set herself not to look to others for help or encouragement, but to do her own planning and pushing. Knowing that her talent lay in her fingers she apprenticed herself to learn dressmaking, and soon became proficient.

I believe it was at the age of eighteen that she heard the gospel preached in a special 'mission' held in her home town, and something in it drew her to the front in acceptance of this dear Saviour. But there was no one to lead Jenny on into deeper things, and so for years she remained unchanged outwardly, though always with a heart loyalty that clung to the Saviour she had received that night. Then there came a time when she became strangely disturbed.

'Whensoever a man desireth aught above measure, immediately he becometh restless', said the wise old monk. A desire above measure had seized Jenny, and not knowing it was His call in her heart, she thought (like most of the rest of us have in our turn) that it was something the world would satisfy if only she could find it. Not realizing it in Scotland, the 'restlessness' urged her to try the new land, and having sisters in Canada, to Canada she planned to come. Thus with nothing to trust to but that heart-hidden Saviour and her own clever fingers, she arrived at the front door of an older married sister. That family soon found they had opened their doors to no mean asset, and so perhaps they were sorry to lose her when that inner restlessness again pushed Jenny on. Out on the Pacific coast, near Port City, was another almost unknown, older sister. Realizing by this time that she carried her fortune literally in her hands, it did not require so much courage to make this second move. Again in a short time she had proved her weight in gold to this struggling little family. Generous with her wages, tireless in her loving unselfish help in the home, quietly 'seeing' things to be done and as quietly doing them, Jenny was soon a very welcome member of the household.

Who that has lived there, but knows the thrall of Canada's Great North West? Was it this Jenny thought would meet that inward desire-without-measure, that under-the-surface day and night calling? Gradually she was beginning to realize that mere things, mere circumstances, even friendships could not satisfy it.

And just as gradually a light was breaking upon her, a light that steadily focussed its rays on the One she had taken into her heart that night in Scotland, but who had been held under the surface, never been allowed to enlarge the place of His feet, simply because she did not know how to let Him, did not even know it was possible for Him to be more to her.

'For still the desert lies
My thirsting soul before;
O living waters, rise
Within me evermore.'

She was working now in an exclusive dressmaking shop in Port City, the kind of place where only the Rich think of entering. Also in Port City there is a struggling little Bible School, and somehow Jenny learned about it. My friend 'Margaret' lives in the flats over the School and is one of its graduates. One day into the office where Margaret was working walked a little figure (Jenny never grew tall). Margaret looked up and saw a stylish young lady with blue, blue eyes looking at her. The carefully marcelled bob, the dainty clothes exactly fitting the small form, all spelled WORLDLY and Margaret thought this was some stranger who had got into the wrong house in this residential district. She was about to inform her cautiously of the mistake when the blue-eyed apparition opened its mouth and asked in Scotch accents if this were the Port City Bible School?

In amazement Margaret said 'Yes'.

The Apparition then said, 'Can anyone attend?'

'Anyone who is a Christian,' said Margaret, eyeing the curls and carefully powdered complexion.

'Could a student live here in the building?' was the next breath-taker.

'Why yes,' gasped Margaret, trying to believe her ears rather than her eyes. 'Not many do but there are rooms above. I live here because I am

employed in Christian work with which the Institute sympathizes, and I help in the office here
occasionally.'

'When could I move in, and begin?' and this
Paradox stood there simply, as if it were the most
expected question in the world.

It was some months later that in faraway China
I received a letter from Margaret. It was a usual
home letter but one paragraph stuck in the memory. 'There's a wonderful little Scotch girl named
. . . (Jenny) rooming here next to me. She is the
pluckiest little thing, earning her way through
Institute and a real girl of prayer. I do wish you
knew her, you'd love her. It's simply grand having
her here.'

Do meteors, before they appear in our world's
hemisphere, send their radiance on *ahead*? I do not
know, but I do know that Second Mile people
have that kind of unconscious power. Something
inside me sprang up and loved that 'little Scotch
girl working her way through' — perhaps because
of the memory of a similar one I had known at
Moody, who is still one of life's treasures.

I knew well the circle in which Jenny was now
moving, and occasionally others mentioned her in
letters, always with love and admiration. The
value of praise depends much on who is giving it,
and I knew that commendation from these people
spoke uncommon worth. But of her plans for the
future I heard nothing; as a matter of fact none of
those most intimate with her were told that for a
year before her graduation she had said 'Yes' to
the Lord's call in her heart for China. Jenny's

acceptance of her Master's will is usually so mat-
ter-of-fact and simple. It is a case of:

'The Master said, "Come follow . . ."
That was all.
Earth's joys grew dim,
My soul went after Him;
I rose and followed —
That was all.
Will you not follow if you hear His call?'

Jenny said nothing to anyone because she knew
she must apply to the China Inland Mission
Council and be 'passed' before she could sail —
and perhaps they would not want a 'nobody'. So
why say anything until one knew? . . . thus spoke
the Scottish in her.

After her graduation I heard that she had gone
with Margaret on a tour of the latter's work, and I
quite took it for granted she would find her place
with Margaret, who loves her dearly.

Every winter there comes a gala event to our far
west . . . the pictures and testimonies of New
Workers from England and America. Very eagerly are the faces scanned and the write-ups read,
because in the spring when designations take
place we invariably receive one or more from the
Language Training Homes. These pioneer districts simply swallow up new workers and gape for
more; during those years when it was our privilege
to receive a few of the Two Hundred into our home
at Old Centre and help them a bit with the initial
'dive' into Chinese life, it was always thrilling to
look over these young faces and make an imagin-
ary choice!

That autumn, as I was eagerly glancing through *China's Millions* one face sprang from the page and challenged my attention. It was a pair of steady young eyes which seemed to have something to say. Just what they said puzzled and so held one's interest; loyalty, courage, goodness were all there, but it was something else, something of promise and of steadfastness, and faintly hanging around was a kind of fragrance of sacrifice . . . yes, that was it. They affirmed a forsaking of all, then a taking up of the cross with a determination to follow the Lamb withersoever He led; there was an *expectation* of suffering in those eyes and an unflinching readiness to meet it. They said, in effect, 'Let us not so stain our honour, as to fly from the Cross,' and this was the promise those earnest young eyes held. I loved their owner on the spot, and glanced beneath to learn her name, then called out with surprise, 'Why it is Margaret's little Scotch girl!' It was *Jenny*.

But the Lord had an even sweeter surprise in store; next spring she was designated to our province, and a few months later Bachelor appointed her to be with us!

*   *   *

I well remember our meeting. One of our 'boys' was the escort who brought both Jenny and a little girl from Moody who was to be stationed two days north. The setting was one of the loveliest imaginable. Old Centre is a famous city on a long fertile plain; the turquoise waters called from their shape 'the Lake of the Ear' stretch out in opalescent beauty to the east, and closing it in on the west are magnificent mountains crinkled into huge ravines and hollows as if some fairy giant had attempted to 'marcel' them. We walked out over the stone-flagged path which slipped between emerald rice fields, until we came to where a large and famous temple spreads itself across the road and calls the traveller to a halt and rest. There we waited, and soon the three figures appeared over a little rise in the path and a call of joy and welcome brought Jenny and Little Moodyite racing forward to see who would reach me first.

My first 'inside' comment was 'My, *how* blue her eyes are!' and then after hearing her laugh merrily I noted, 'She may be solemn earnestness at the centre, but the surface knows how to ripple into fun! *Good*. She'll make a dandy missionary sure enough.'

There was no stiffness in the merry party that wended its way back to supper. Jenny and I had long ago heard of each other and came from the same circle of friends; Little Moodyite had the latest news of the beloved old school to tell us, and 'our boy' had just got himself engaged so he was obvious prey for everybody's fun! But such delightful gatherings may not be prolonged in the more important duties of missionary life, so a few days later the group broke up and Peter (who is a girl despite what you are thinking) claimed Little Moodyite as her own and marched off with her to their station.

There was a change for us too, for we had been

given that one desire of pioneer hearts, permission to 'open up' a city for Christ. John had already been there while escorting two of our boys towards the town which they in their turn were to enter for Christ. On his way home he had stopped off and managed to rent a ramshackle Chinese house in 'Old Street' city. He warned Jenny and me that it 'wasn't very nice; if I had been willing to wait for a month or so, and then make another trip there, I might have been able to get a better house — and I might not have been able to get any whatever!' John had often been committed the task of renting the houses which our young workers were to occupy in their pioneer fields, and our experiences in getting into new cities was that after a house was found and the lease just about signed, the landlord would suddenly back out, appalled by the furor his renting to a foreigner had aroused. It was best to have all tightly witnessed and signed before one left the owner to the lashing tongues of his relatives and neighbours.

Jenny and I laughed at John's worried look. Had there not been definite prayer that he would get a house on *that* trip? And who wanted to delay several months in order — possibly — to have a nicer home?

'Well then, there's another thing. I think you girls had better wait here while I go over there and get the carpenters and masons busy, and get things a little ship-shape. Then I'll come back and get you and we will move as a family.'

Again there was a howl of derision which brought a grin to John's face, for after all it would be much nicer to have everyone along. So he shrugged his shoulders and said, 'Well, if you regret it, don't blame me! I advise you to wait here until the place is clean and ready for ladies.'

So on the appointed day we started to trek west. Oh that *start*. Horsemen that promised to come at six am did not arrive until ten am, and then it was discovered that we had a load more than was calculated, so they had to send out of the city for another horse, so after a long forenoon of 'waiting to go', Jenny and I with Baby (for God had made us three by that time, with a little daughter) started off, leaving John behind to 'wait for that horse'.

Travelling in inland China! Oh the petty trials of the flesh, the stiff-backed won't-be-hurried, won't-do-it-differently of the Chinese coolie or muleteer! And then when you do get going, how the sublime beauty of God's wonderful mountain country cools your heated spirit.

One memory of that trip which stands out is the scratch of a match at four-thirty, and Jenny lighting her candle for a 'quiet time' with her Lord before the day's clamour could sweep in and interfere.

Then came the afternoon when we finally reached the little heathen-locked plain and arrived at the entrance of Old Street itself. All the way down the main street John hurriedly reiterated the bad points of the house into my ear, so afraid I would be disappointed — and he always can tell, even though I try to cover it up!

Just as the river came in view we turned over to the right, crossed the village commons and were in our future 'home'. It proved to be a small court-yard with three surrounding wings and a crumbling wall on the fourth side. In one wing smoke was pouring up to the roof from a big Chinese stove (the Chinese tenants had not yet moved out!), of the main wing one wall had collapsed in the middle like a small boy with a stomach ache and a rough log was bracing it up to keep it just standing. The third wing had no proper floor upstairs, and everywhere was soot and dirt and darkness. Chinese fear sunlight and fresh air, and as much as possible had been done to keep out these intrusive brighteners. One room was so dark you could not see *anything* when you poked your head in, but oh, the smell of mould and the feeling that small 'creatures' were in abundance!

Upstairs in the main wing was a little lighter by reason of wooden windows that *could* be opened, but everywhere soot and dust hung and lay thick. The north wing was to be Jenny's but was only half floored; the east wing which was to be ours was then used as the family worship hall. Each evening, before the family moved out, the land-lady would come up, light the incense and lamp, kneel on the grass mat, knock the wooden fish with her little hammer in order to arouse the gods, and mutter her prayers. How the taunting truth of Elijah's words would silently rise to our lips some-times, as we watched her tireless knock-knock-tap-tap. 'Cry aloud, for he is a god; either he is talking, or he is pursuing, or he is in a journey, or peradventure he sleepeth and must be waked!' But we dare not do more than think it, because she was an earnest Buddhist and sarcasm would only have set up a permanent barrier against us and our Christ. For such, the only way is to love them persistently until the strangeness of Christian living awakens a hunger in their hearts and they come of themselves and ask, what is the difference? Then one may tell them, and add 'And this Saviour does not need a noisy banging to draw His attention to us. Such is His love that He cannot forget us a moment of the day or night, and He has even said, '*Before* they call, I will answer'.

When at last the Chinese did move out and carpenters and masons arrived, such a mess as we all lived in! As it was a pioneer place people were afraid to come as our servants, so although we did have some help we also did a lot of the cleaning ourselves. And always — so quietly we hardly were conscious of it — John's and my comfort was taken care of *first*.

I can see Jenny now, as one morning she appeared on our flat, head tied up in a white cloth, apron on and broom in her hand. By that time we had dug out the blocked-up windows and hacked a third one out of the mud wall, so we could see somewhat.

'What are you going to do with this?' and I eyed the broom suspiciously.

'Sweep down your roof!'

'But, Jenny, your own roof needs the same! Let's go and do yours first!'

'Mine can wait. The floor isn't finished anyway, and besides you're three and I'm only one. Mine can be done any old time, it doesn't matter.' That was always it; Jenny's comfort 'didn't matter' . . . and in spite of expostulations somehow she got her way.

So I hunted up a cloth to tie over my own hair, and together we stood and looked up at that roof! It had no ceiling so we were gazing at the under part of the mud tiles themselves, and they were black with the soot of years (incense burning every day and doubtless other fires) and moreover were festooned with long streamers of dust like rusty-black moss, spider webs and moth cocoons adding some variety; on the whole I suppose it was rather picturesque!

'I've got it,' said Jenny, 'I'll just mount on that high incense table they've left there and then I can reach that side of the rafters. Here goes!' and in a second she had climbed on to a low cupboard and from there was just about to ascend to the table when the humour of her position caught her, and with a roguish grin she posed there a second — one foot on the table and the other on the cupboard, the broom flourished in her right hand. 'Pride goeth before . . .' she began chuckling, but go no further when bang! boom! crash! I felt the whole house shake, things fell on and around me like rain. Remembering the ricketyness of the old place I concluded that at the least the roof had collapsed, and covering my face with my hands I stood waiting to see if any particular tile was going to escort me into eternity. However, as all was quiet after a moment I ventured to open my eyes; there in the middle of the floor, in the midst of dirt and debris, sat a small figure with a face as sooty as a chimney sweep's and two blue blue eyes of astounded amazement looking out and up at me from their black circumference. Then the next moment, the roof (it was still there!) rang with shrieks of laughter.

By this time John, having heard the crash, was upstairs in a bound, but seeing the blue-eyed 'chimney sweep' in the middle of the floor and realizing that no one was hurt he too leaned against the wall and roared. Unknown to us, the long heavy incense table had been resting one foot on a rough stone; Jenny's spring had caused it to topple over, carrying not only her, but the small cupboard too, and the heaviness of the crash in that shaky dwelling had 'swept the roof' for us truly, in showers of soot and chunks of mud. When finally we could control ourselves the soot-besmeared 'chimney sweep' assured us she was uninjured, but as her garments were torn it was necessary for her to go and change — so she departed chuckling all the way down the stairs.

Thus with a willing merry heart she stuck by and helped us all through those busy trying weeks. Finally whitewashed walls, plaster, a mended roof and straightened walls began to reward our labours. We were just at the point where we could start to do some real evangelistic work when a letter from Bachelor arrived. Another missionary had had a physical breakdown and must be escorted to the coast; as John and I had both been needing medical attention ourselves he thought it was wisest if we would be that escort. The question of course was, what to do with Jenny? It would be a most valuable experience to spend several months alone among the Chinese but Bachelor said he would never think of asking such a difficult thing of a young lady; so he supposed the best arrangement would be for her to go and live with the nearest married couple until our return.

Sometimes I have seen, as it were, the Lord standing behind Jenny's shoulder, with one hand of love resting there, and with the other silently pointing to a 'second mile'. How solemn are the blue eyes as she broods thoughtfully out into space while talking with Him in her heart. There was no sign of struggle, but after a while she said, 'You may write and tell the Super that I'll stay right on here alone. It will be a valuable experience, as he says, and it is not wise to leave this newly-opened field unmanned.'

Carefully we tried to explain to her what such a decision would involve; no other foreigner within three days' journey, she as yet unable to speak the language, no Christian to help or sympathize with her (there was a cook, but her life did not commend her profession of Christianity), and we must be gone some time — it turned out to be four months. Jenny was quietly firm; 'It's better for me to stay,' was all she would say.

So we had to leave her, a little figure standing at a curve of the road with tombstones of a Chinese graveyard on either hand, and the sunny plain behind her. Was it symbolic — one small living figure among all those dead that lay so heavily, so stonily around her? Would that weight of heathenism crush her? Nearly two years later a Bethel Band visited this place and said they had not met such 'stony' hearts since Shanghai! Old Street adds deep ignorance to its blind heathenism — few people can even read on that little plain. Stones . . . graves . . . and one young heart with the Word of Life — who would win?

It was there I saw her again on our return. From one hill-top I looked across and on the opposite hill, seated on a tombstone, was a small girlish figure which got up and waved delightedly at my halloo. In another second we were both racing down to the bottom where a creek flows rippling over rocks; a leap across and I had her in my arms.

Not much would she ever say of those long four months alone, of the awful isolation, seeing human beings but not being able to converse with them, the monotony of the days, the dragging slowness of language study, the groups of Chinese visitors who examine everything with impudent freedom (or so it seems to us who have been brought up to respect personal privacy), the longing to tell them of the Saviour who is theirs for the taking, the blundering awkwardness of one's tongue and the hot humiliation when an earnest effort meets with ridicule. On the surface, the 'stones' were still stones, but constant prayer from an unswerving young heart had done much to loosen some of them, as we found when we returned and began to preach the word of their salvation.

A casual remark dropped by someone long after, poured in a stream of light upon that four months and then I knew, though she would say so little to loving questions, that Jenny had indeed not 'offered unto the Lord that which cost her nothing'.

* * *

We had brought back with us two more young lady missionaries — a splendid gift of God to our great west. My father, hearing of the three living with us, laughingly nicknamed them 'Faith, Hope and Love' and asked them to choose which should be which; Jenny instantly chose Love — 'because,' she said, 'it abideth forever'. So with these three we passed a happy and somewhat eventful summer.

One evening in the autumn we gathered around the dinner table very gay and happy indeed, for two of our boys were out visiting us en route further west! Into that merry group a bolt fell, and again it was a letter from Bachelor.

'Seeing the important centre of Eternal Prosperity has had to be vacated,' read the superintendent's letter, 'it has been decided to ask Misses Jenny and Hope to occupy it, and we advise that they move immediately.'

Now Jenny and Hope are both dears, but they are very different, born at opposite points of the temperamental compass in fact. They just naturally came to different conclusions about things; Jenny believed, for instance, that the best way to

work was to go out alone among the people, and
Hope with equal sincerity believed that it was
most unwise for an unmarried foreign girl to live
alone among heathen, that the Lord's own
method had been to send His disciples two by two.
And with other questions little and large it was the
same — how could two such different tempera-
ments *pull* together?

In our Mission we are not forced to work with
anyone we do not wish to work with, and the girls
could have refused; but the Mission are most
prayerful in making designations, and we were so
glad that neither of them showed by word, glance
or deed that there was anything but quiet acceptance of it as the will of God.

There is nothing in the ordinary life of the
homelands which quite resembles this particular
trial which can often face two young missionaries.
Picture two girls, neither as yet able to speak much
Chinese so shut up to one another and unable to
escape through the usual channel of ministering to
the people. Language study can be a soul-sapping
monotony. In a paradoxical way, work among the
people is refreshing; true, there is almost always
much fatigue, but the giving out of spiritual
strength in one's preaching necessitates a corres-
ponding intake from the Lord Himself, which
refreshes the spirit no matter how tired the body
is. But at the language study period the constant
stuffing of the mind with sounds and 'characters'
is a very real physical drain, and without an outlet
the soul feels stale and barren. Confine together
two young people in this condition, people who

did not choose each other as companions and would rather have avoided it — then leave them alone with no other congenial fellow being as a refuge to 'fight it out', and it is no mean battle! Chances to walk 'the second mile' are of almost hourly occurrence until any romance attaching to such an idea is quite gone, and one becomes only conscious of a mad desire to 'break loose' and do as one wants to, say what one wants to!

A ridiculous cartoon exactly illustrates this situation.

"Stop following me!"

Notice the obviously vigorous temperament of Fish No. 1; how galling to be forever followed around by the inane smile of Fish No. 2! Fish No. 1 has 'broken loose' in impotent wrath, 'Stop following me!' But HOW impotent! Where else can

Fish No. 2 go? It would be just as bad to proceed in the other direction, and always be running into Fish No. 1 . . . much better to skulk along behind his indignant tail!

Under such circumstances one can imagine how little things, which at home would seem too puny for a Christian to notice, suddenly grow into importance. I remember once being left alone with a missionary who had fallen into lazy habits of speech, such as saying *git* for *get*, and *gittin'* for *getting*. This simple little thing, which would have been passed by with a smile at home, gradually became important, gradually became distinctly offensive. One took oneself to task for being fretted over such an insignificant matter, when there were so many noble qualities to admire in the speaker, but private scolding made no difference, something within resented it until one found oneself actually screwed up to meet *git* and *gittin'* at meal times when escape was impossible. A return of the family or an influx of visitors relaxed the strain until now it is even forgotten who the offender was . . . but the way the molehill grew into a mountain remains a vivid memory.

*   *   *

Anxiously we waited and prayed for Jenny and Hope. Would a 'breaking loose' moment come? What would happen?

'Said the Captain gently, "The second mile's long,

But I walk with you when you seek not your own." '

Under the heat and pressure of this unexpected chosen Cross, whose 'own' would they seek? Those who seek 'their' own invariably end up this way, 'You go your way and I go mine!' But Christ does not walk that road.

Months later the answer was revealed by a visitor to Jenny and Hope's station, who told us: 'Those girls meet every day for prayer together for the local church! They pray for every member they know, every day, no matter how long it takes them, and it usually takes over an hour.'

What joy that remark brought! For it showed them seeking *His* 'own'.

'*I* walk with you when you seek not your own.'

That One was walking with them in the midst was soon evident. News drifted over of revival in a little body of villagers out on their plain. Then after about a year, the Bethel Band paid a visit and no place in our West gave such response as this city, notorious for years as stony-hearted, materialistic and fruitless from the missionary standpoint!

Hope wrote to us joyfully, 'You will have heard from Jenny of the times of blessing we are having here. It almost seems unreal, it is all so wonderful . . . if many more people keep coming on Sundays we will have to get more benches.'

And later Jenny herself: 'Yes, I *am* glad and rejoice daily in the way God has blessed and is blessing "Eternal Prosperity". For the past year Hope and I have had special prayer time after lunch daily . . . and our special request long before the Bethel Band came was for a work of the Holy

Spirit to be done among the educated people of the city, *especially the teachers*.' One of these school-teachers, named S——, had been converted and was taking a remarkable stand for his Lord. Writing later of this particular man, Jenny said, 'We heard of Teacher S—— attending a swell dinner and holding the audience while he gave his testimony. He told us of someone saying to him "I hear you have entered the Jesus religion . . . what's the matter . . . do you think you are going to die?" He replied, "I've been dead already 30 years!" and went on to explain how.' Later still: '. . . a message came to Teacher S—— from the school authorities (who said it was also from the City Magistrate) to the effect that if he did not give up the Jesus religion and allow bills to be posted all over town to that effect they would bind him and lead him up and down the main street. He replied by letter, "You may bind me and lead me down the main street: you may make a cross and crucify me on it, but I will not give up Jesus." No more has been said — that was three or four days ago — and the other teachers have nothing to do with him. His determinate stand is going to mean much, I am sure. He prayed so nicely as we met after service yesterday — said he knew that persecution was only to burn up the dross and bring him out as gold. God grant it in his life.'

Is the 'second mile' ever walked without reward? Never. Our sufferings, our heartaches may never be known to any but Him; we may finish our course and still be 'a nobody' in everyone else's eyes (though I really think Second Mile People are too rare and shining not to be noticed sooner or later) but there is *always* the 'Well done, good and faithful servant' from a Voice beloved beyond any other's; there is always the smile of Jesus, 'Heaven's sunshine'. Our second mile need not be spectacular; Thomas Ragland said, '*Two* talents gained a "Well done!".'

*   *   *

And now I have before me a last picture, a little vignette, which illustrates so clearly and so simply 'the second mile' life, especially in its common-place phases, where you and I may also walk it.

Once we were travelling over a mountain on a cold autumn morning. We were so high that the clouds enfolded us, cold wet gray mist, they seemed. I was chilled to the bone and got out of my chair to walk but even then felt the depression of that piercing encircling fog. Finally John, ahead, called back, 'We are going to descend now! Cheer up dear, we'll soon be in the sunshine.' A moment later, 'There! Isobel, look! There is the plain! Down there!' Looking where he pointed I saw a break in the gray cloud that enveloped us, and through it, framed as with silver mist, way, way down, hundreds of feet below lay a long sunny plain, with tree-shaded little hamlets here and there, and merry little brooks and creeks singing their way across it, and resting comfortably against the opposite foothills a big busy Chinese city.

It was to that very city that Jenny was called, at

one time, to 'fill in' for a while until its regular missionary could return. And now I want you to look with me through that frame of silver mist, at this little vignette. In that big city, in a little upper room, Jenny is sitting, elbows on desk, face in hands, blue eyes looking earnestly out through the window. Is it the sun-drenched plain they regard so thoughtfully? No, it is the One inside her heart to whom she is talking — for Jenny is in a dreadful muddle, an unthinkable mess, a tangle of circumstances over which she seemingly had no control — whatever will she do? It is this way. Long ago Mish. A. lived in this house and owned some furniture here; then she became independent of the CIM, moved away and sold her belongings to Mish. B. Mish. B. in turn, later on, sold to Mish. C., whose place Jenny is 'filling'. But Jenny was told none of this history, and one day along comes a letter from Mish. A. saying she is coming back to work in this city and would like her old furniture back which she had lent to Mish. B.

Jenny happens to be using that very furniture, but believing she has no right to it, says nothing but turns it all over to Mish. A. on her arrival. Then comes a letter from Mish. C. (who has heard of it) in which Jenny is told that Mish. A. must have suffered a lapse of memory, that the deed of purchase can be produced and that *that furniture must be returned*.

Now Jenny knows that Mish. A. has not been purposely dishonest; she is well on in years, poor and lonely, she lives very simply and has no other furniture or comforts. Demand these back and

what a predicament that poor soul is in; besides
. . . well, wouldn't she be wounded to be told she
had 'mis-remembered', when it had been done so
guiltlessly!

So there she sits, a little figure in this big mess;
the solemn blue eyes are steadily gazing out on the
plain, but inside she is saying, 'What would You
do, Lord?' The answer comes softly down the
centuries — does He ever answer otherwise than
thus? — 'If any man compel you to go a mile, go
with him *twain*.'

The blue eyes lifted . . . 'All right, Lord. Thank
you. That is what I wanted — *just to know*.' And
Jenny goes out, quietly calls a carpenter, tells him
to copy that set of furniture, make new ones
exactly like it, and say nothing but charge the bill
to her. And this at a time when her own funds were
rather low.

*   *   *

For nearly two years Jenny and Hope lived
together in a harmony that the Chinese say was
unique. Then to Jenny came the fulfilment of a
'heart's desire'. She had long silently cherished a
wish to be sent to Lisuland to work; it was a
longing that seemed hopeless at first, for no single
woman had ever been sent into that difficult
mountain country. But prayer opens many closed
doors, and after much 'knocking' — very private-
ly, on her knees — this 'door' was opened to her.
She was designated to the southern district, the
Mission saying they had decided to make a trial of

single woman workers in Lisu work, and Jenny was to be their first experiment.

A lively young nurse, whose name means 'Purity', was sent to be with Hope, and two weeks after her arrival Jenny set off with a group of delighted Lisu 'coolies', for the land of her heart's desire. She sent me a joyous note, 'Goodbye! I hope to *die* in Lisuland!'

5

STAR — WHO JUMPED OFF THE EDGE OF THE MAP

'Hast thou no scar?
No hidden scar in foot, or side, or hand?
I hear thee sung so mighty in the land.
I hear them hail thy bright ascendant star,
Hast thou no scar?'

— Dohnavur.

THIS 'BRIGHT ASCENDANT STAR' in the modern Christian firmament — known and beloved on more than one continent for her writings — lives with her husband, Pioneer, in Lisuland, so far north of Jenny that it would take almost two weeks to span the intervening space.

One day, eight days to the south of Star's field, in the little town of Old Street, John was reading a letter from Pioneer. It was a vigorous call for help. The field to which Star and Pioneer had gone was many days north of the old original district Bachelor had worked. This northern part of the great Salween canyon is even more inaccessible, wild and mountainous, but Lisu hearts were prepared to receive the Gospel with joy, so the two brave

missionaries had gone in to live among them. But
the work spread far beyond their ability to cope
with it; the Mission listened to their need sympathetically, but there were no workers to send.
Desperately trying to teach enough to give these
young inquirers something solid to stand on, lest
they get discouraged and step back into darkness,
Star and her husband decided to separate till help
should come. She was to stay all alone among the
Lisu of their present district, while he went six
days north where Lisu were turning to Christ by
hundreds.

Sitting in the rough chapels of Lisuland, during
an evening service when the only light is that from
the pile of flaming pine chips, I have often noticed
the difference between the sappy chips and the
drier ones. The sappy ones have a clear transparent look about them, you know them at a glance.
Put one such on to the burning pile and the flame
will reach out for it and lick it up at running speed;
and often, as I sat and watched such a chip, I
noticed that when the fire reached the heart of it it
would emit a slight explosive sound, like one great
cry of agony; then shortly after the yellow fury has
it in full flame, and soon it is only a charred stick or
gray ash.

Those clear transparent 'sappy' chips always
remind me of Pioneer. He is not afraid of the fire, if
by flinging himself onto the pile he can light up the
way of salvation for a lost soul. There is desperate
determinedness about him at such times. We have
seen him fling himself upon an area of Satan's
dominion and claim it for Christ, and when the

'fury of the oppressor' is aroused it only causes him to stick tighter. The hosts of evil, vexed to madness, attack him on all sides, and even appal him, till like the burning pine chip, he lets out a little cry, 'I'm afraid I can't stand it!' — but he always *does* stand it.

How deep is the heathen darkness of that northern part of the canyon we cannot tell, but a letter from Pioneer, written while among the as-yet-unconverted villages, seemed fairly to shudder with the horror of the powers of wickedness. 'At night,' he wrote, 'I can hear the carousing of the heathen Lisu. Their drunken laughter has a demoniacal ring to it that turns the blood cold — this is a terrible place; never have I felt the rule of evil in such strength. I can hardly stand it.' But being Pioneer, he did stand it, stuck till he had pushed through. The Chinese laird was infuriated at his tenacity, even going so far at one time as to threaten the people if they gave him any food. Still however, all along, Pioneer remained at his post, gladdened on the one hand by the hundreds of Lisu who were turning Christian, and simply dauntless as to the 'fury of the oppressor' that opposed on the other side.

By 'Chinese Laird' you must understand the one who owns, legally, the mountain land which the Lisu plant with corn for food. In those parts feudalism still exists, the Chinese landowner being the 'laird' and the Lisu being the serfs. These heathen lairds suddenly learn that their subservients, whom they scornfully treat as mere animals, are learning to read, have thrown off demon worship and are worshipping one 'Jesus', whom the foreigner has introduced. Jealous and angry lest their hitherto unchallenged control be weakened, they begin to persecute and threaten.

Opium is not supposed to be planted in China now, and if it is, a tax must be paid. These Chinese lairds make a good profit out of the opium tax, and so when they hear that Lisu Christians will not plant the drug any more, they are enraged and demand double the tax from those who will not plant! What though it is rank injustice! Who would ever dare the hardships of the road in, to come and investigate? One Consul tried, but losing his food load where the narrow road broke and fell into the river under the weight of the mule, he had to turn back at just the fringe of the great northern canyon.

So the exultant lairds threatened those dear Lisu Christians around Star, and although she is a good linguist in both Chinese and Lisu, what is a woman to a Chinese official? Of no effect at all. So down to Old Street came a call — would John please come up and stay in Star's district until the opium season was over? His very presence would be some restraint, and any help which would lighten the bitterness these dear children of the soil were enduring, would certainly be worthwhile.

The SOS fell into prepared hearts — a recent sorrow had made us tender and caused us to look up to the beloved Master to try and ascertain if this had a deeper meaning than was on the surface; was He trying to direct our lives into some new channel? Then from one source and another, the need of this great new Lisu district began to come to us, and before Pioneer's letter arrived our eyes had begun to look to those northern mountains and watch. Originally we had been designated to 'tribes', but my ill health and other potent reasons had prevented us; we had thought that after furlough perhaps the way might open. But while our eyes were still 'unto Him', this call came and seemed to settle it.

'I must go,' said John, 'and I would like to take you with me. I would like to have you try the hardships up yonder in person, before we offer to the Mission; a visit would test out your physique whether you can stand Lisuland or not.' So, leaving Small Daughter in Faith's capable hands, for it was best not to subject her to such rough travelling, we both went.

*   *   *

There is a river, a green snarling, death-dealing river, which cuts its way savagely through gigantic masses of rock which humans call 'a mountain range'. It is as if, in antediluvian days when God purposed the green plains and valleys of Chinaland, this 'back of beyond' became the monster Dump Heap of all the excess rock and debris from the levelled ricefields. Through this chaotic, concreted pile the Salween river has tried to escape, boiling and thrashing its way with impotent fury at the strength of the cool resisting granite. It has dug out, chewed out, a twisted canyon of many hundreds of miles in length, with steep lonely sides rising thousands of feet above the petty snarl of the green waters.

Into this inaccessible, unlivable mountain dump of rock were driven the hunted aboriginal tribes as the greedy strength of the civilized Chinese overpowered and threatened to annihilate them. And here, on the topmost sides of that Great Canyon, live our dear Lisu, scratching the hard face of the bare mountain for soil enough to grow the corn which is their staple food.

So John and I set out northward, travelling for nine days, with occasional rests in remote Chinese towns where a testimony for Christ was needed. It was a great moment when we arrived at noon at a Lisu village, and John, who had been there three years before, called me to the steep roadside and pointed out the rest of our day's journey. We stood on one brow of a mountain; at our left was the long river canyon with its immense peaks piercing the blue. We were on the right bank, as you face up the gorge, but 'the bank' is just a succession of monster mountain-steps with chasmy sides, down and up which the puny little human dot must travel in order to 'go up' the canyon. The hill dropped away from beneath us in one of these abyssal ravines, and curling laboriously back and forth in the brow of the opposite mountain was our path.

'Star lives just around that corner where the trail disappears!' said John, grinning as he watched my face. How often he had tried to describe those mountain vastnesses to me — but who could really make them visible to one who had never seen?

I glanced slowly around, catching my breath at the silent magnificence of those wonderful peaks and crags with their mighty dropping sides; then the loneliness and isolation of that back-of-beyond Dump Heap smote me.

'And a *western woman* lives on that stony face "around the corner where the trail disappears"!'

'Yes.' John was still grinning with joy at my awe. 'And you and I have still to go down this mountain — and it's some drop, you'll find — and up that path before we reach her today!'

Late afternoon found us rounding the curve which was to bring us to Star's fellowship and home. 'There is the village over yonder, don't you see those three little huts? That's her house,' pointed out John. 'I wonder is she at home?' Eagerly we scanned the tiny huts for a sign of life.

'Yes, look Isobel! Someone's standing on the roof watching us!' Sure enough, a man was coolly poised on the roof of the lower shanty; because they are built against the steep mountain sides, you may walk from the ground onto the back of the roof of Lisu houses, so it is often a favourite place to sit and work.

Suddenly we saw a red sweater flash in the sunlight between two of the huts. 'Yes, she's home!' we cried joyfully, 'no Lisu could be rich enough to possess a sweater.'

Then we both felt queer. How did one meet such a well-known person? (For we were stran-

gers.) What would she be like? We had often heard
of her devotion to the Lisu; perhaps she would not
be much interested in anyone else? Would she be
regal, dignified with a preoccupied air? . . . she
was an author, after all.

John was troubled for another reason. An old
Hebrew tradition says that Eve was very loqua-
cious, and that Adam used to call her his 'never
silent bell'. Sometimes — I say it sadly — John is
tempted to sympathize with Adam.

'Now listen, Isobel; you know how you *talk*. Just
listen to me for once and try to control yourself!
Remember who she is!'

Isobel heaved a sigh at her 'strong weakness',
promised to be good, and tried to conjure up the
dignity that should befit a newly-made 'senior
missionary'.

By this time the red sweater was flashing in and
out of the curves of the trail, and before another
word could be said a happy girlish voice called
out, 'Oh how good to see white faces again!' I
found myself smothered in a warm loving
embrace. The heartiness and joy of our welcome
were unmistakable, and the unaffected sweetness
and youthful heart of our hostess took us by
surprise, for we had pictured her as middle-aged.
Beneath such loving friendliness Dignity found
herself forgotten, folded her wings sadly and dropped out of sight, while John was soon groaning
within him as he listened to my tongue wagging
along merrily like a puppy-dog's tail.

The shanty which was Star's home was a long
one-storied place, with bamboo matting for walls,

partitions and floor, and wooden shakes for a roof. It was decidedly rough, but tidy and clean, and somehow looked home-like and good to our eyes. Star had been expecting us weeks before, she said; we had been delayed, not able to get carriers and with no way of informing Star, so she had given us up. 'So many say they are coming in to see us, but none ever arrive!' she said gaily. 'Yours are the first white faces I have seen for nearly a year, except my husband's, of course. But I haven't seen him for over a month, and when he left he told me to be prepared to go without seeing him for three or six months!'

Prepared to go without seeing your husband for three to six months! And taking it all as a matter of course! She was not in a big American city surrounded by loving friends and relatives, but on this lonely steep mountain side, beyond 'the edge of cultivation', with only primitive Lisu for society and help. In my heart I stood and saluted her.

Talking and laughing, she seemed to radiate joy as she busied about getting us a delicious little afternoon bite of fresh muffins and hot tea; for Star is a splendid cook among other things.

Evening brought in Lisu boys and girls, whose free assurance revealed that they knew they were always welcome guests. 'Each evening they come to keep me company,' Star smiled. 'Some nights we study Chinese, at other times learn a new Lisu hymn or have a Lisu-script reading class — always there is something to do.' She might have added, 'and always I waive my own comfort and live for them,' for we saw her, after a busy day of

Bible translation, interspersed with odd interviews with deacons over church problems, sitting
down with these Lisu young people in the evenings. A pink spot of fatigue in each cheek would
urge her off to rest, but with cheery smile and
indefatigable earnestness, she taught them to a
comparatively late hour.

We had been at Rock Dump only a day or so,
when one morning in through the open doorway
walked three strange-looking Lisu; their costumes
and features were different, one having a decidedly Hindu cast of countenance. As usual they were
too bashful to accept the invitation to sit on chairs,
so just squatted on the floor at Star's feet while she
questioned them. What a picture that group
made! Star's dark eyes were sparkling with the joy
of the tale which was unfolding to her ears, and the
three brown-faced men in picturesque white and
red costume told their story with oriental casual-
ness, their sweet musical intonations falling
pleasantly on the ear. Out through the open doorway behind them loomed up mighty peaks with
crests of snow dazzling white in the morning
sunshine.

Star questioned and listened, and every now
and again threw in a hurried interpretation to give
us the thread and progress of their narrative. They
had come over those great gleaming mountains,
come from Burma in fact, for those same mountains are the China-Burma border, called on the
other side 'The Burma Mountain Wall'. They had
been travelling seven or eight days and had come
for the one and only purpose of getting Lisu

teachers to return with them and instruct them
how to worship the Lord Jesus. But the thrilling
part of their tale was that eleven years previously,
in their Burma Lisu village a woman had come
under the power of a demon which made her
tremble all over and give forth strange tidings.
'God has a son named Jesus,' spoke forth the
demon who said it was 'God's Daughter'. 'He is
the Saviour, and one day God is going to burn up
the world, but if you trust in Jesus, God will take
you to heaven so you will not be burned. If you
believe in Jesus, you must keep one day in seven as
worship day, and not smoke opium nor drink
wine.' (As far as we have been able to ascertain
since, this woman had had no contacts with
Christianity at any time.) The villagers were so
frightened at this that eleven families tore down
their demon altars and have trusted in Jesus ever
since. Years passed, and one day a Lisu who had
been across the huge mountain range to the Salween canyon to trade returned with startling
news. He said that the Lisu over there were also
worshipping one 'Jesus', but they had books and
teachers to tell them how. This was wonderful joy
to the faithful little band, and immediately the
decision was made to send for these teachers and
books, and also learn the ways of their God. Twice
an attempt was made to do so, but both times the
parties failed to get over the Great Pass. At length
in March 1934 these three young men started
forth with purpose not to be frustrated, and now
even though they had 'to bite their way through
the snow of the Pass', they had crossed and here

they were. 'We have no books and no teachers. Please help us.' They had been worshipping thus for *eleven years*.

'They say they've brought their own food and are going to stay till they can get a teacher, no matter how long they wait!' — and Star shot us a glance of triumphant joy, for the staunchness of Lisu hearts never ceases to thrill her. But it was quickly followed by sadness — 'There is no one free to go.' (Later two went and there is now a little Church there.)

The men dismissed, we fell to talking over the work, and before long we had told her how God was laying it on our hearts to offer to the Mission for this field. 'How happy my husband will be!' she cried. 'We've just not known how we could manage if someone did not come to help us soon! Oh I wish you could stay right on, and didn't have to go back!' But responsibilities cannot thus so easily be flung off; it takes a long time to get an answer from Headquarters back to these inland parts.

We had not been at Rock Dump many days when a letter arrived from Pioneer, which said that he was badly needing her to help him cope with a Short Term Bible School which he was hoping to hold. Laughing gaily she read out to us a portion: 'If our guests have arrived, can't you leave them to take charge down there, and come and help me?'

'Imagine such a thing at home! "If your guests have arrived can't you leave them alone and come to me?"' then she stopped and said merrily, 'Well, what will I answer him?' Soon it was decided that since the Lisu pastor and ourselves all spoke Chinese, we could be left with him as interpreter without any cruelty, and it was much the best for her to join her lonely husband.

But before she went, a question which had often been in my heart was answered for me. The question was this — do people who seem to make sacrifices quickly and easily really care as deeply about things as us other folk, who seem to find it so hard? Isn't it just that they are naturally ascetic, that their hearts do not cling to the things of this world like our hearts do? I knew Star as a writer, had now met her as a missionary, but I was curious to know her as a *mother*.

On the wall of the shanty hung a few photographs, among them one of Star and Pioneer with their two boys, taken the year previously when the parents had visited our Mission school at Chefoo. I knew that the older boy had not seen them for four years. From six to ten is a long time for a mother not to see her son — how did Star ever stand it? To me it had been simply agony to leave Baby Girl in order to come in and make this trip, and that was to be only a separation of a month or two. Was it that Star's love for the Lisu was greater than her mother-love, and helped her not to care? Or was there a sorrow that she did not let people see, a something under the bright cheeriness which ached and hungered for what for His sake she was denied?

'Hast thou no scar?
No hidden scar, in foot or side or hand?'

One may not pry into another's sacred privacy, but it is sometimes good for us to know the truth, lest we excuse ourselves from the Cross saying it would cost us much more than it costs others, that we are more delicate and tender and we must receive special consideration; thus falling into the pit of self pity, we can miss His pattern for us.

It was not difficult to get Star to talk about her boys — she was full of stories of their young days at home in Lisuland, and once said quietly that when she came back without either of them, to this lonely Rock Dump, she did not know at first how she could stand it. She passed quickly on to some other matter and we did not dare ask her to linger, but we had caught a sense of a silent Companionship which had gently offered to fill the empty aching places. There is none but He can do so.

However, later on at the table the conversation once turned upon Chefooites, and their enforced absence from home.

'Most of them,' said Star, 'get to see their parents at least once in two years. We did not know till we got there that our David had gone the longest . . .' here her voice broke suddenly and with eyes swimming in tears she finished with quivering words . . . 'of any of them,' and quickly rose and turned away.

'. . . can he have followed far
    That has no wounds? no scar?'

A holy reverent silence filled the little shanty as that mother-heart offered up its bleeding tears to the One who 'fully understands in our weakness'.

'God never wastes His children's pain' said one

who knew pain. But He has a pattern for each of us, which He longs we might attain, a perfection so lovely that it is easily worth a few years of cost, a few 'hidden scars'.

'Why should I start at the plough of my Lord, that maketh deep furrows on my soul?' cried out the valiant Rutherford, in days of long-forgotten suffering. 'I know He is no idle husbandman; he purposeth a crop.'

And so, because not even God can give us at the same time a 'crop' and an unfurrowed soul, Star dried her tears and quietly raised up under the weight of the Cross again. This 'crop' was not for herself, for her own vainglory; oh no, it would not be worth a scratch let alone a 'furrow' if that were all; it was *for Him*, that He might 'see of the travail of His soul and be satisfied'; and it was *for them*, that they might have 'Life, and Life more abundantly'. As for what she might or might not get out of it, long experience had taught her that that was in perfectly safe hands.

All too soon the morning came when Star left us to go north to Pioneer. As she passed on to the trail ahead, riding her white mule with her Lisu bodyguard of faithful carriers, John turned to me and said, 'Isobel, you think you've done some travelling in your time but you have yet to tackle a road that can touch the one she's facing now! I went over it on that trip three years ago and believe me, it was a hair-raising experience more than once! Why, some places the trail just disappears into a ledge at the top of a precipice, and all you can do is to cling to your mule, close your eyes and pray!

And she has only Lisu to accompany her — well, I'll say she's brave!'

*   *   *

Months later word came from Headquarters that, after prayerful consideration, it had been decided to approve John and family moving into Rock Dump Canyon, but that whether they settled in the south or northern district would be left for Pioneer to decide. It did not take him long. 'South' had been discovered and opened up first by one we can only call Trail-Blazer, for here he and his plucky wife made the first missionary home and stayed till her health broke down and they had to withdraw. Their enforced desertion of the field acted as a challenge to Pioneer and Star, who had volunteered to leave their old beloved Lisu district (Jenny was sent there later) and come in here to fill the emergency. The 'emergency' turned out to be a permanent call, and, as I have already told, Pioneer flung himself through the narrow-wedged opening into the 'North' and there he decided to remain.

'You take the south', he wrote to John. 'The south is partly broken in now, you can get food and stores through much easier there than up here. Here there is no market of any kind for ten months of the year and we will have to grow what we are to eat. Come in as soon as you can. I hardly dare leave here for fear the Chinese laird thinks he has driven me out, and then he'd turn his rage upon the poor people; else I'd come down and help you get settled in.'

As a matter of fact, later on he did come down once for that purpose, and waited day after day, leaving Star alone in the North; and day after day we did not come. No telegraph here, very irregular mail once in ten days — how could we tell him that John was ill and we had had to go for medical help? But that is the next story.

Finally God brought us in, and this is being written from Star's old shanty home. Star herself is up that tortuous rocky canyon, on the other side of the river. To get there she had to cross a 'rope bridge', which is merely strands of bamboo twisted into a rope and flung over the river, across the canyon. To get you across, the Lisu tied you onto a bamboo slide, which slides over the rope; when tied, you shoot head first down to the middle of the rope, and wait there with the hungry green waters beneath you until a Lisu on that side slides down, attaches a rope to you and hauls you up to the other bank.

The rope decays every so often, and if you are on it when it breaks you are doomed. The stiff sun-dried coils unwind with great rapidity and twine around you, then in that octopus-grip you are spun down and held under the green waters until you have departed this earthly tabernacle — and perhaps much longer. This will help you to understand a letter I received from Star just a few weeks ago. She wrote:—

'I must say that I feel a wee bit as though I had jumped off the edge of the map. For there is no way out of this place except to go dangling across the river on a rope. However, I seem to have all I need to eat, plenty of servants and heaps of friends, so I guess it doesn't matter whether I am on the map or not!'

6

DOCTOR — THE UNPROFITABLE SERVANT

PERMISSION TO MOVE INTO Lisuland, boxes packed
to go — and John ill! Was this of Satan? Or had
God been merely testing our willingness, and did
He mean us to have furlough first after all? Long
ago Bachelor had once said, 'God never leads us
into blind alleys', and how often had those words
helped us to be steadfast at a time of ignorance and
indecision. Oh, if sometimes the Lord would only
appear and shout in unmistakable tones 'To the
RIGHT!' — or to the left, whichever was His will
— just so one would *know*. But maybe then we
would allow our ears to get dull, trusting to the
loudness of His shout? He prefers to keep us on the
qui vive, with every nerve and sense keenly recep-
tive to His faintest whisper, in other words to
make 'minute-men' out of us like those of the
American army who must hold themselves in
readiness for service at any moment.

Summer had brought four reinforcements to
our west, of whom one was an answer to many
prayers — a young doctor.

During the summer, John had been having serious symptoms and although different medicines had been tried, nothing helped. Knowing that both families at Old Centre, where Doctor also lived, were expecting the small sons which now enliven their homes, we were reluctant to add to the burden of housekeeping by John going there to interview Doctor. But finally it became too serious and he had to go; then a week later, I got a telegram ordering me to come also, as it had developed into real dystentery, and also there was an operation which Doctor deemed imperative.

At the same time a happy letter from Pioneer arrived, telling of his decision to leave Star to guard the northern work while he himself came down to help us settle in. 'He must be there now,' I groaned, 'every day watching for us to come around the corner; and I can't telegraph him, or get word to him for perhaps the better part of a month. And all our things packed to go north-west and *we* have to go *east*. Oh *why*?' But He that sitteth in the Heavens just laughed quietly; He knows His children's needs better than they do themselves. 'God is content to wait, because He reigneth; man must be content to wait, because He believeth.' He had prepared one of His 'good things' for us. But when God turns us out of the main road into the unexpected and strange, it seems to be human nature to expect the worst.

It reminds me of a time when we were still at Old Centre, and a number of our boys and girls were home. It was discovered that our beloved dog — a big burly fellow, half Tibetan and very faithful — was sick, and someone declared Castor Oil was the only thing to save him. We were discussing it in his presence, and at that dreadful word he got up and slunk off. Immediately chase was made and after quite a scramble, one of the boys caught him and brought him to the fatal bottle. I can see the pair now, the tall man stooping to grip the hairy neck and dragging him along with all his four legs obstinately stiffened in rebellion, tail between his legs. Poor fellow, I sympathized — that's just the way I approach Castor Oil too, but we had to save his life.

Strong manly arms grabbed each limb of him, another boy forced open his mouth while one of us tipped out the oil. At the first drop that hit his gullet all tension ceased, and when the spoonful was at an end he extended a greedy tongue as far as his astounded captors would allow, and licked that spoon gratefully on both sides! Needless to say we collapsed with laughter, and the freed dog went from one to another wagging his tail and begging for more of that delicious nectar. He had expected to be punished, and got feasted instead!

And isn't that the way with us? God suddenly lays His hand on the scruff of our necks and right-about-turns us, and immediately we look for punishment. Thus with stiffened legs we are ungracefully dragged up to what He has prepared for us — only to find it is a feast!

John and I were more tired than we realized, tired in spirit as well as body. Spiritually there was a feeling of desperate determination to go on, even though it meant falling in one's tracks. Against this jaded weariness God sent a fresh young enthusiasm which swept us like a cool breeze. I can best describe the effect on us by an illustration of travelling in Lisuland.

The trails in that mountain country are not level but simply up and down; at one place a village on one side of the canyon can hear the beating of the gong for chapel in a village on the other side — yet it takes nearly two days to get from one to the other! Plodding up the steep dry gravelly path with the sun beating hot on your back, you feel as if dry dust were inside as well as out. Hot and weary, with parched throat and tongue, you reach an elevation, a pine tree by the road edge or a jutting rock, and stand there a challenging target for the brisk mountain Breeze. He never fails to pick up the gauntlet, and rushes against your jaded dustiness till a cool freshness seems to slip through all parts of you; you drink him in by the lungful, grateful for the stinging whip of him, for the wholesome thoroughness of his working. Then you turn again to the hot gravelly ascendant path, feeling as if you have been renewed, inside and out.

It was of the exhilarating effect of Doctor's fresh, vivid devotion that John wanted to speak, when finally I arrived at Old Centre and at the loved one's bedside. For he was still in bed, but the thin whiteness had already left his face and he was quick to say that the dysentery had already gone — 'Just getting stronger now for the operation,' he added cheerfully.

'There is no need to worry over this delay, dear,'

he comforted as the afternoon dusk filled the little room. 'It is from God, I am perfectly sure, Isobel. I can't tell you what a blessing Doctor has been to me and I feel God is going to give us something new, spiritually.'

*   *   *

'There is nothing so kindling as to see the soul of man or woman follow right over the edge of the usual into the untracked land — for love of Him, sheer love of Him.' — A. Carmichael.

The heart of the Eternal is forever reaching out toward mankind SEEKING true worshippers, that is how Jesus put it. S.D. Gordon phrases it this way: 'God . . . has a hungry heart. He is hungry for us, for you and me . . . He is hungry that we would be really friendly with Him. The word commonly used for this is fellowship . . . That inner hunger of spirit, that yearning within, that eager wistful reaching out and up, it is an echo, only an echo. And the echo is always less than the original. It is an echo of the longing, the yearning, in the heart of God for us, for each one of us.'

As each human soul is formed, its yearning Creator takes care to make for Himself a place within it; a space which only He can fill, and which must remain empty and dissatisfied until He is invited to come in and occupy. All of us have such a place in our natures, but it would seem as if God's hungry heart creates some every generation in which the 'space' is deeper, wider and more persistently calling for Him. These, all down the ages, have delighted to term themselves His lovers, and they are marked by the fact that He truly is the consuming passion of their lives.

It was said of Habbukuk, 'He alone of the prophets was more concerned that the holiness of Jehovah be vindicated than that Israel should escape chastisement. Written just upon the eve of the captivity, Habbukuk was God's testimony to Himself.'

Put beside that, this from Ramon Lull of the thirteenth century, 'Foolish Lover, why doest thou weary thy body, throw away thy wealth, and leave the joys of this world, and go about as an outcast of the people?' 'To honour my Beloved's Name,' he replied, 'for He is hated and dishonoured by more men than honour and love Him.'

The recognition of that empty space can come very early. Amy Carmichael says, 'My first memory as a tiny child is this: after the nursery light had been turned low and I was quite alone, I used to smooth a little place on the sheet, and say aloud to our Father, "Please come and sit with me".'

In England six years ago there was another young heart of kindred likeness. Six feet tall, broad shouldered, fair, with deep set eyes blue as the sea, something about this boy whispers of the 'Norsemen' that most probably were numbered among his ancestors; there is a touch of the Viking also in the daring and aggressiveness of his personality, and the wanderlust which pulsates strongly in his veins. But deep within, covered from a stranger's eyes, there was always that hungry 'space' which God had reserved for Himself, and its emptiness ached to be filled. 'Earnest', 'intense' are words the world throws upon such a one, as it passes him by.

He was very carefully trained and educated away from God from the start. His mother is a very intellectual woman, who took the gift of her children very conscientiously, but she is thoroughly 'modern', and that word in quotation marks will tell those of us who have tasted all that modernism has to offer, without any other explanation, how that the lad kept *just missing* the God for whom he was hungering. He was told of the Bible as a book upon which many people were fanatical; he was taught that the Christ of Calvary was only a splendid visionary whose tragic death ended all; he was informed of other religions of other peoples in order that he might 'cull the best religious thought' from all the highest intellectual efforts of mankind; for this same reason his dear mother conscientiously made him read books on philosophy, theosophy, Hinduism, Spiritism and other cults that appeal to the mind, but there was nothing in any of them that could fill or satisfy the yearning 'space' within.

The Christ, Doctor told us, even as an historical personage only captured him with painful sweetness, and every thought of Him was as a wooing, a great enthralling which made the lad love to linger about Him in thought.

And then there came a time when 'the space' would be neglected no longer and in his ignorance and hunger he began to form the habit of 'quiet times' night and morning, when all his soul gathered itself together and plunged, Viking-like, into the unknown — seeking, searching for God. 'I got,' he told us simply, 'so that I could not do without my quiet time, night and morning.'

At twenty-one he was a student in the medical college of London University, and there he met another student, the Christian son of Salvation Army missionaries, working in India. When summer holidays came this friend invited our Viking to spend the season with him at his home in Norway, for his parents had returned from India. The invitation was powerfully attractive; it was true that his parents had planned an educational visit to the Continent for Viking, those holidays, but earnestly he pleaded to be allowed to use the money to go to Norway instead.

'All that the Father giveth Me shall reach Me,' said Christ, and the 'reaching' time had come, when the Saviour meant to span the distance between, and take unto Himself, His own; nothing in the universe could have checked that meeting in Norway, so it is not surprising to learn that his dear parents yielded to the lad's desire, and there on that northern coast 'the space' was filled at last.

Coming home on the boat, a mere untaught babe in Christ, he tried to lead one of the officers on board ship to his newly-found and peerless Master. No thought of 'What will He ask me to do, if I surrender?' ever bothered him; instead there was just the joyful, 'All this for me? All this for me?' and an urge that would not be quieted to share what he had with others.

Now in that medical college there was a band of orthodox sincere Christian students, who met to pray regularly, and they had been asking God to save one of the other students. And God had answered their prayers. What if they had asked for twenty? or more? But they had asked for one, and God had given them one, and for a time it seemed as if he was almost one too many! For that new convert, instead of coming in and sitting down at their feet, as any young convert might be expected to do, to learn of them how to walk the Christian pathway with measured step and decorous mien, this babe in Christ gave them one glance and then started on his own to do the most unheard-of things! Why he started *having prayer with his patients*, and dealing with them about their souls! — *sick people*, you understand; but some of them got saved. Conventional orthodoxy was annoyed, and just a bit offended; but the young doctor went quietly on.

When he finally started to operate, he sought whenever possible to have prayer with the patient in the ante-room, just before the latter was carried into the operating theatre. And one day, when he had finished, he distinctly heard an 'Amen' behind him! Turning around he discovered a nurse there, and on inquiring found she was a Christian. This led him to search for other Christians among the nurses of that hospital, and finding some, he formed a prayer meeting among them, which was still being conducted the last he heard.

Then came his call to China, as a missionary to

carry the message of his Lord's Cross and Resurrection, and that He died for all. A China Inland
Missionary hurt her finger at a summer conference, and through this little incident the 'call'
came.

'In this God-caused, designed concurrence of
events, in themselves ordinary and natural, lies
the mystery of special Providences, which, to
whomsoever they happen, he may and should
regard them as miracles,' says Dr Edersheim.

The Chinese territory which borders Lisuland,
and to which I have referred as 'our west' is some
two weeks distant from the nearest hospital or
medical help, and in all of the whole province
there was not one foreign dentist. Sickness swept
down upon us and the field lost two young missionaries whose vacant places seemed to gape at
us. Friends at home, widely separated, wrote that
they were praying for a doctor to be sent to us. We
read their letters with weary unbelief — they did
not understand the difficulties. For one thing, so
few doctors offer to the CIM that our hospitals, in
other provinces, cannot get enough of them, much
less spare any; then he would have to do without
hospital equipment, and what doctor wants to
work with 'makeshifts' and homemade contri-
vances? Then — this was not an obstacle, just an
extra — we *did* need a dentist too, for bad teeth
cause bad health.

One friend, evidently wishing to help God out
in such a difficult matter, wrote us he was praying
that the Almighty would cause the doctor to
marry a lady dentist! (When we told this to our

Viking how he laughed. 'Rather limits me, don't you think?' he said mischievously.) But the Heavenly Father had prepared a physician-surgeon-dentist all in one man, and the faith of the friends who 'did not understand the difficulties' was abundantly answered.

But we have not heard all that John had to say to me that first afternoon of our reunion at Old Centre. He was filled with his new friend.

'Doctor is a man of prayer, dear, just like Bud. He prays with every patient he treats, and deals with them about their souls before he allows them to leave him. Even with me! Every morning and evening he comes in for prayer together, and we are having rich times!' John's face glowed.

'He reminds me of Bud in other ways too. Doesn't hang around the sitting room chatting and having a good time with the crowd; in the evenings when the rest of us are having a social time together he will be out in the garden, or on the city wall, praying. That's the price he pays, dear. Oh, I'm going to learn all I can from him while we're here' — and John's pale face was tense with determination. Moreover it seemed from then on that things began to happen, and a tide of human souls was let loose on us.

For six weeks we were plunged in the most intensive soul-winning campaign that heart could desire. Doctor laid aside his study routine, and taking advantage of the presence of senior missionaries (who had more language) he offered to see patients for one hour a day.

That 'one hour' became a joke to us. Chinese

are blissfully indifferent to time-schedules, and
when there is a chance to get skilled medical
attention they instantly become afflicted with
deafness, and simply cannot hear you when you
tell them that Doctor has already a houseful and
cannot see any more sick folk today!

There there were two groups of people to whom
Doctor never had the heart to shut his door — the
boy High School students, and the soldiers. At
this particular period thousands of soldiers were
bivouacked in a large barracks only about a mile
outside the city's north gate. How long they would
be there was, of course, a matter beyond calcula-
tion and Doctor, often passing their encampment
on his daily walks, yearned to get an opening
among them. To this end he and John prayed in
their morning and evening times together.

It was a red-letter day for me when I was first
invited to join these prayer sessions. Around
John's bed we knelt, and Doctor opened up his
heart with a prayer which swept one right into the
Saviour's presence, and was so intimate one
almost felt one was eavesdropping. He prayed for
souls, for revival of the local church, but first for
himself that Christ might have him, body soul and
spirit. 'I deny myself, Lord,' he cried, 'I take up
my cross and I follow Thee. I *choose* to be poor,
lonely, despised and suffering, even as Thou
wast.' It was a prayer that made one catch one's
breath. One thought of the brilliant gifts of the
young life that so prayed; clever, well-educated,
and with graceful courteous manners that immediately attract, and a whimsical wit that makes

him socially popular. Were all these to count for
nothing? Why should such a one *choose* to be
lonely, despised and suffering?

Months later that question was answered when
I stood on a slim beautiful ridge in Lisuland and
looked at a tall splendid pine tree, with half its
noble heart hacked out by Lisu knives. The sap
oozed and dropped like slow tears from the huge
wound. A stab as of pain startled the indignant
words, 'Oh, what a shame!' But the great beautiful tree, its dauntless head held straight in the air
which it perfumed on all sides, seemed to pity my
ignorance, seemed to be given voice, and spoke to
me this parable:—

'Do you indeed begrudge my heart and lacer-
ated trunk, my friend? Turn and look at that
foot-path behind you. See how it skirts the steep
mountain side, look where it meets that jutting
gray rock, which is too unyielding for primitive
pick-axes. The trail disappears into a mere thread
as it goes around that crag — you know how you
hold your breath when you have to cross it at
noonday. But what if you had to go over there in
night's dark hours without a light? Lisu cannot
afford lamps, you know; all they have to illumin-
ate their path are pine chips. Think well — if one
of your beloved Lisu were on that perilous trail at
a dark hour, how would he find his way safely over
. . . *without the heart of me*' and then I understood.

There are stumbling feet groping over dark and
dangerous paths of sin, in this world, and they can
only have their way lit home by the burning
heart-sacrifices of others, who *know the road*. If

young hearts will not be given up to be burned out
for God, those stumbling, darkened ones must
forever perish. Before many days were over, he
who had prayed that prayer and one who had
heard it were to stand by the death-bed of a young
life that had missed its footing in the perilous way
because there was no lamp to show the road . . .
the Light had not reached her soon enough. Can
the pain of that scene ever leave us? No, dear noble
pine-tree, and young gifted life, we do not begrudge your wounds. Who would be heart-whole
while the cry of those who have missed their
footing, pierces the night?

> 'O Father, help, lest our poor love refuse
> For our beloved the life that they would
> choose,
> And in our fear of loss for them, or pain,
> Forget eternal gain.'

After a time our prayer meetings were thrown
open to the whole 'family'. The Bethel Band were
due to visit Old Centre and there seemed so much
to bring before God. All through our weeks of
evangelistic effort those prayer meetings (usually
around John's bedside) were our strength and
great joy. 'Prayer' says Dr Edersheim, 'is to lay
our inner man wholly open to the light of God in
genuine, earnest simplicity, to be quite shone
through by Him'. They were 'shining through'
experiences, those evening prayer seasons, when
outside the small lamp-lit room, the fierce mountain wind would come whirling down the steep
ravines of the hills which guard Old Centre on the
west, and with a demoniacal howl hurl itself

against the house where we knelt, making it shiver. One felt the powers of darkness, but dimly as a sort of background to the warmth of the Presence which shed a glow on us all, and made us loath to lift our bowed heads, at the end of the hour, and open our eyes on this earth again.

One matter of intercession was that we might get an entrance into the big barracks outside the city. They had been asking for this before I came, and the evening before John's operation something happened. One of the young missionary couples went for a walk — their first evening stroll together since baby son was born. As they returned several soldiers were walking just in front of them, but as both groups approached the Mission compound one of the soldiers suddenly cried out, held his stomach, doubled up and then fell down *right at our doorway.*

Our first intimation of it was Doctor bursting into the room and shutting the door, then leaning his back against it, breathless, as he tried to tell us. 'I came for your advice,' his words came in quick short gasps. 'I want you to pray about something. A soldier fell down at our door — has perforated gastric. If I don't operate, he will die in a few hours.'

His face was glowing with excitement (he is a born surgeon and had never done 'a gastric ulcer' all by himself before!) but he came forward gently, sat down by John's bed and took his hand in his.

'You see', he went on more quietly, but still obviously thrilled, 'it seems rather funny. There is the operating room all set — Nurse has everything all sterilized and ready — your operation could easily wait over a day, if you are willing, and this might be the opening into the barracks we have been praying for. What do you think?'

We thought it best to ask the only One who really knew, so the family were called in, we knelt around the bed and asked our Father to tell us — was this from Him?

Years ago Bachelor had taught me a prayer-formula to use when suddenly obstacles seem to insist that we make a curve or detour from the straight path ahead. I found it so efficacious that I in turn taught it to John, and it has become a part of our lives. It is this — 'Lord, if this be from Thee I accept it, but if it is from Satan, I refuse it.' (Long years later I found it in John Bunyan, in this form: 'If it be of God, let me not despise it; if it be of the Devil, let me not embrace it.') This prayer formula works perfectly *if* the one praying is thoroughly honest and means cheerfully to accept or cheerfully to do without the matter under consideration. We use it too with 'heart's desires', for often a strong heart's desire may not be from God; and yet it may be too, and if there is that foundational honesty and surrender to God's will this prayer formula will work well. We used it that night, and with it cast out two 'fleeces'. One was — if the military authorities gave an unconditional consent to the operation, we would say operate; the other — if after an hour or so we were *all* united in feeling it should take place. By the time mentioned both fleeces said, 'Yes, go ahead and operate'.

My, what a bustle ensued! Nurse (she is especially well qualified and experienced, indeed Doctor used to praise her and call her 'House surgeon'!) flew like a white bird up and down stairs, along corridors and in a little time the home-made dispensary was all in its white drapery and everything in place. One was in charge of the boiling water supply; another, in one of his wife's white nursing aprons, was to help her as she gave the anaesthetic, and also to hold down the patient if he proved 'naughty'; I together with medical officers from the army barracks made a thrilled audience, while John (not to be left out of it) on the other side of the partition held the overflow of Chinese men guests in conversation around his bed.

A gastric ulcer operation in a private house in *inland* China, with only two experienced helpers! A Petromax lamp was rented and hung over the wooden 'operating' table; Doctor displayed with a grin some mutilated forks and gave them a distinguished name which he and Nurse understood if we didn't, and so on. Only happy confidence filled the atmosphere, and just before Soldier Jo went under chloroform prayer was made for him in Chinese, with the heathen medical soldier wide-eyed at such proceedings in an operating theatre! It was all over in an hour and then prayer was made again, asking God's blessing and seal on the work done, and that not only his life be saved, but his soul also. Then an improvised stretcher was put together, and Doctor helped to

carry his own patient downstairs to the room
below John's, which had to do for hospital ward
for some weeks.

By this time it was about midnight, yet still
there remained something that Doctor wanted to
do. While Nurse and the others were cleaning and
tidying up next door, Doctor slipped into John's
bedroom. I can see him now as he came in, quietly
closing the door behind him. His hair, wet with
perspiration, clung to his brow, and the young
face was so lined with weariness that he looked
two decades older than he was; but his eyes were
shining. He stood and gazed at us a moment, his
thoughts going over the success of that hour just
passed, then in tones of deep joy he whispered,
'Praise God!' Taking John's hand in his, he knelt
down at the bedside and started to pray his thanks
and gratitude for help received; what a prayer it
was! Not a vestige of credit would he take for
himself, not a thought of personal praise or glory,
he just took all such honour and tumbled it off his
own shoulders, heaping it at the feet of his Lord,
and knelt and worshipped and adored. One of his
favourite sayings, when people try to tell him what
his skill and kindness have meant, is this — 'Well,
praise the *Lord*! When we have done our best, we
are still unprofitable servants, aren't we?' And
'unprofitable servant' was all he would allow
himself that night; the credit for a successful and
difficult operation under most handicapping circumstances was all given back to the One he
serves, to the One who prayed many hundreds of
years ago, 'the glory Thou hast given Me, I have

given to them.' Yes, that glory is really and truly only His, but He loves to share it with us, and it silently filled that little room that evening, and we all three drank of it.

And Soldier Jo whose 'tummy' was so successfully sewed up? And the door to the barracks? God found his way into the heart of each. At first Jo was a bit obstreperous; I can still feel the angry kick of his foot as he refused to let me take off his shoes when he was to go to bed! And I can still hear the angry howl with which a soldier-guard leaped upon him and whipped them off regardless! That howl and the roughness of the action showed only too plainly how human underlings were treated in that army — 'love' in its true meaning, is unknown there.

But it was 'love' that tended Jo day and night, for our dear Nurse was unselfish kindness itself, and daily efforts were made to give him an understanding of the Truth. Every day the army supplied two soldiers to sit with him, and help to tend his wants, and to these also was the gospel preached. We were now invited to the barracks; soldiers thronged to our house and daily, for a while, a band of us went into the barracks to preach and to heal the sick. The joy and thrill of those days is beyond description. Perhaps I can help you understand by just picking out one soldier from the many whose lives were touched.

Every missionary should come to the field with two weapons for his warfare against heathenism. In his left hand he should wield the weapon of prayer, and in his right the Sword of the Spirit, which is the Word of God; the one to be used in battling with the unseen principalities and powers, the other for the visible flesh and blood, and the barriers which it throws up against him and his message. These weapons must always be of one certain make — no other is efficient. That of prayer is bedded in a hilt of the metal of faith, and is engraved all over with these words, 'Not my will, but Thine be done'; for effectual prayer must spring out of faith, and out of a whole-hearted consecration that will say, 'Yes, Lord' at any moment, and in reply to any call from Him.

The right-hand weapon used in visible warfare is a delicate blade, so beautiful and precious in workmanship that it reminds me of that famous and exquisite sword, the Excalibur of Arthur. As to the blade itself, there is only one which can 'pierce to the dividing asunder of soul and spirit' (the Holy Writ), but Excalibur had something more than its blade, it was 'rich'

'With jewels, elfin Urim, on the hilt,
        Bewildering heart and eye — the blade so
                                                            bright
    That men are blinded by it . . .'

It was that shine of bewildering glory, which, in battle, downed men's hearts before it ever touched their bodies. So it is with the sword-of-the-right-hand. For every 'Yes, Lord' engraved upon the left-hand weapon of the missionary, there appears a jewel of LOVE upon the hilt of the right-hand blade, a jewel of deep passion for Christ, until the Sword of the Spirit is one dazzling glory of constraining LOVE. This is the Excalibur of the right hand, a burning love for the Lord, and for the souls He died to save, and at its centre is His own two-edged Word, the message of salvation. It is this sheen of love that breaks down barriers of race, religious prejudices, everything — and leaves the heathen heart open for the naked blade to enter — the convicting work of the Spirit of God. I have seen it so often . . . dull care-worn 'closed' faces meeting that shining touch of one of Christ's lover-of-souls, suddenly open up with a great wistfulness, a shyly dawning light of welcome. Oh what a powerful weapon this missionary-Excalibur is . . . the Word of God, bejewelled, effulgent with the love of Christ.

Doctor came to China well-girded for warfare; the weapon of Prayer had long been his dear familiar, and his love for the people we have never seen excelled in any missionary. 'By one who loveth is another kindled' said wise old Augustine. No man was too dirty or poor but Doctor's arm went lovingly around his shoulders, and the physical revelation of Christ's life often spoke more strongly than the worded explanation. It was so in this case.

One evening after a long and hard day's work, Doctor went in to see Soldier Jo, who was now up and convalescing. Nurse was not at hand for she had had to return to her station, so I went in also to see if any help was needed. The little room was dark, except for the glow of a coal fire in an iron bowl the Chinese call a 'fire basin'. Soldier Jo was seated there brewing some tea for himself, and for a young soldier lad who was his attendant that night. The latter got up immediately on our entrance and insisted that Doctor take his chair — and as he did so, the soldier Laddie sat down at his feet. Doctor is tall and big-framed, but he is not physically strong, and he was very tired that evening.

Soldier Jo yielded his chair to me and then squatted in front of me, and we began to talk with the firelight throwing its red glow over the four of us. I asked Jo if by now he had taken the Lord Jesus into his heart as Saviour, and he said 'Yes', but so weakly that it led to conversation on that dear Redeemer and His death for us upon the Cross. Jo's eyes were riveted in attention on my face, but I was conscious of a drama going on to the left. As usual, Doctor had slipped his arm around the soldier lad's shoulders, and the latter had turned to him a look of amazement which gradually shaded off into wonder and then into wistfulness. The big foreign doctor so to condescend to him, a mere common cipher of a Chinese soldier? To him those in high places had only shown harshness, callousness, contempt, but his boy heart was hungry, and here was one to whom his highest officer bowed respectfully, actually putting an arm around his shoulders! He was too thrilled to listen to what the foreign woman was saying, but with the wonder of this new friend glowing in his face, he shyly reached out and touched Doctor's knee. Finding he was not repulsed he snuggled up close and whispered, 'How old are you?'

'Twenty-six,' came from the shadows into which Doctor had disappeared as he leaned back wearily in his chair.

'Shut up and listen!' growled Jo who was simply drinking in 'that sweet story of old' and who had been distracted a moment by the whisper. A touch from Doctor urging the same brought Laddie to attention, and he found himself listening to an account of another Life, a Life so selfless, so loving, that instinctively the boy felt it must be linked up closely with that tender pressure around his shoulders, and he became enthralled. As I went on, approaching that most sacred spot of Calvary with all its wonderful, beautiful detail, the earnest gaze of Soldier Jo, the wistful boy eyes of Laddie, the red firelight and dusky shadows seemed to disappear and we all stood upon a faraway hill with its torturing crosses; we shivered as the noonday sun turned to black darkness, we trembled as the earth shook beneath our feet, and we thrilled as we heard the cry of 'Finished!' ascend in triumph up through the sorrowing heavens to the Throne of God. Then the peace of that Easter morning stole in upon us, and the heart-bursting joy of that tender assurance of the risen Lord, 'Be not afraid, it is I!' made us draw in our breath: as words ended, a solemn silence filled the shadowy fire-lit room. There was One standing there, unseen, holding out His nail-scarred Hands to two heathen-dark hearts, and all thoughts were upon Him. Forgotten in the radiance of this Greater Light was the human love which had first revealed Him to Laddie's amazed gaze, and now his boy eyes were looking out in wistful hunger into the shadow-filled room.

'Little Brother, won't you take Him as your own Saviour tonight?'

The words startled Laddie into attention.

'But I can't read!' he said as if standing on the outside of a barred gate.

'You don't need to,' came Doctor's voice from the dark shadows, '*He is a Person*, all you need to do is to KNOW Him, and receive Him.'

'Little Brother, do you know Doctor?'

'Yes,' he replied, turning to gaze at him with a smile of shy love.

'But you say you cannot read, how can you know Doctor? Don't you see that taking Christ as Saviour is just the same as taking a new friend into your heart? Only this Friend must become Master. The more time you spend with Him, the better you know Him. It is not a question of reading, but of *getting to know Him*, and then obeying His voice. When we talk to Him we call it praying. Won't you talk to Him now and tell Him to come into your life as Master and Lord?'

The young face considered it thoughtfully a moment, and then looked up and smiled, 'Yes'.

So there in the firelight Laddie, guided by us, talked to Him of Calvary, and asked Him to 'come in and rule'. Oh the joy of the quiet that followed that prayer! Where are they now, those two common Chinese soldiers who faced Christ that night — Jo of earnest gaze and Laddie of the wistful eyes? I do not know, only I know the Friend they invited in that evening says He will never forsake those who trust Him. 'He never yet put out a dim candle that was lighted at the Sun of Righteousness.' Dim candles are they both, illiterate common soldiers of China, ordered from place to place with no settled abode, no Christian friends to help and teach them. We who love them can only commit them to our Faithful Master, and pray for them.

As I went upstairs to John's room, I wondered just how genuine Laddie's profession had been — so soon does Satan send Doubt to nip at the heels of Faith. Had he really understood? Had he said 'Yes' just to be nice to us? Just to please us . . . thus yelped the Heel-Nipper.

Our last Sunday at Old Centre John had been asked to preach at the big noon service. He had spoken — poured out his heart — the Sunday before, but no one had publicly responded to the invitation to receive Christ. During this week our daily prayer meetings focussed on this last message, but Saturday evening came and found John in despair.

'Please go and tell them to ask someone else,' he said to me pleadingly, 'I've tried all day and I simply can't get a message. Have had so many people wanting interviews with me too. I can't get any definite message, can't seem to *get through*', and he groaned. But I remembered a similar Saturday in my own experience, and knowing that the agony of weakness had reaped a harvest of glory for the Lord on the following day, I comforted him, and we prayed and sang — for sometimes praise pushes through when petition seems to have knocked in vain.

That Sunday noon John went into the pulpit with just one thing before his eyes — Calvary. The men's side of the church was thronged with soldiers, and at the end he again gave the invitation, asking for raised hands from those who would then, or had during the last few weeks, taken Christ as their Saviour. A hand went up. I leaned forward eagerly to see who it was that had the courage to proclaim himself a Christian in front of so many fellow soldiers. I gave one look then sank back in my pew crying in my heart, 'O thank God! It's *Laddie*!' For so it was — his face looking up at the man in the pulpit was simple and sincere, and his hand raised awkwardly, was visible to all. In a minute or so Soldier Jo's hand went up too (that day he looked pale and weak, not so earnest as Laddie) and then a hand here and there, each one being received with much gaping and nudging of elbows by the heathen soldiers.

Then from John, 'Will all of you that mean it, come out from your seats to the front?'

My heart failed me, 'Isn't that asking a bit too much?' But no, out walked eleven soldiers and lined up in front of the pulpit.

'Now all of you get down on your knees right there, and pray Christ to forgive your sins' . . . ('Oh surely, John, you are going too far! Oh poor boys . . . see how their comrades are standing up to get a better view and look at their grins! Oh, will they do it?')

Yes, down on the stone flags went eleven pair of

knees, then a blue shadow slipped down the aisle, went in and knelt among them — it was Doctor. With his help and John's (who also went down among them now) each of those men publicly prayed to Christ for salvation, though I must admit that one or two looked as if Courage was reaching for his hat to flee! But they all stuck to their guns and stayed till their names were registered and they were dismissed.

By this time I was on the organ stool facing the gray uniforms, and as they stood in line before breaking up, it so happened that Laddie and another soldier boy whom I had also pointed to the Lord in the weeks just passed, were standing together at the end of the row nearest the organ. As the line was dismissed and they turned to go, each boy (unknown to the other) bent his head and shot a quick smile at the one on the organ seat. Both smiles said the same thing — 'I knew you'd be glad to know I *meant it*!'

'Will there be any stars in my crown?' sings an old hymn. Who would care for stars when they might have such warm human smiles lined up in heaven awaiting them! '*Ye* are my joy and crown of rejoicing', said Paul.

Laddie's story is only one of many who came for healing for themselves or others and went away with the knowledge of something better. Doctor's cures made him famous in a few days and people thronged for attention. But he insistently, relentlessly, refused to see more than he had time to deal with concerning their salvation. I and others preached to those downstairs who were waiting

for an interview, and often John from his sick bed
had dealt with one or another as they were leaving, while Doctor and Nurse prayed with each,
seeking to lay the emphasis on faith in the only
true God. So we sought to saturate them with the
gospel, and leave them without excuse of ignorance.

One other scene comes up before me, and I may
not but tell it. It was a case that Doctor lost,
though through no fault of his own; but one cannot
forget her for she left a scar upon the heart.

One morning at breakfast we were summoned
to two cases at the same time, each of which was
an attempted suicide through swallowing opium.
The first was a girl of sixteen, and it took all
Doctor's skill to bring her back for she was far
gone, but God purposed to save her life and she
was restored. As we left that house the second
man, a poorly dressed fellow, was waiting for us,
and said, 'Now you must come to my place!
There's a woman there who swallowed opium an
hour or so ago.' As we went he proceeded with his
story. 'She is a poor tribeswoman who has had
some trouble with her relatives-in-law and ran
away from them. She came to our place late last
night, and asked for lodging; she deceived us' (the
man was bitter with anger) 'and did not tell us she
meant to commit suicide in our house, just asked
for lodging; and then this morning my wife caught
her swallowing the opium. It isn't fair! We are
poor people and have no money for her coffin.' In
China, if a stranger dies under your roof, you are
responsible for his burial, and this man was filled

with wrath at the trick played upon him. There was no sympathy for her troubles — heathendom shrugs its shoulders at a broken heart.

For broken-hearted she was. I never found out the details of her sorrow, but as she was married, it is not hard to guess — probably a hard and cruel mother-in-law. She seemed to be nearly thirty years of age and was of the peasant class. She was easy to restore but took the medicine unwillingly. (Her death was caused by re-swallowing opium, secretly, later on in the day, after we all thought she had been saved.) It was such a blank face, blank and dull with despair, a face from which hope had fled. As we looked at that desolate hopelessness, as we saw the timid way in which she tried to refuse life-restoratives (timid because she evidently thought we'd beat or rough-handle her, if she didn't take the medicine, and yet with a heart quite determined to die) we wondered how we could ever strike through that dead despair in order to challenge her consciousness to listen to what we had to say. Her mind was quite clear, but her heart was broken and 'life' had died within her. We wanted to reach *her* not just her physical ears — how stab that 'her' alive again, alive enough to listen to what we had to tell her? We used the most amazing words that such a one could ever have heard. We said, 'Sister, there is One who loves you, called Jesus'.

Such a blow was sufficient, and for a moment we thought we had her, for the soul of her leaped into her eyes with one great appeal, and then Reality gripped it dead, and the blankness closed

over it and she murmured wearily, 'Puh ai. Puh
ai.' (Literally 'not love, not love' but she meant
'No He doesn't. It's not so.')

Reality that had only known a loveless past and
looked upon a loveless future told her we were
creating this big lie in order to deceive her back
into life, and so she shook her head, and in a tired
voice said, 'No love . . . no love.' We left her sitting
there, restored in body but still dead in her heart
— and then later we learned how she had tricked
them and now lay dead in body too. And of her
soul? Our hearts just cannot stand to follow that
thought.

But let her words, symbolic of millions of her
fellow sisters, haunt your hearts, as they have
haunted mine, 'No love, no love!' *That is why she
died*! She couldn't live in this cruel world without
it, and she had ceased to hope that there was such
a thing for her. Do you think that the heart of Him
who died for love of her and others like her, was
not crucified afresh, as she passed into Eternity
with 'No love, no love' upon her lips and scarred
upon her soul? And who is responsible for the fact
that she was not told in time? (Lucky Laddie to
have learned it before hope was dead.) Not Christ.
His part is 'finished'. He has said plainly — and
named no exceptions — 'Go ye into all the world
and preach!' And by His Holy Spirit He has also
said, 'How can they be saved except they hear?
And how can they hear without a preacher?'

Those Christians who love themselves better
than Him, better than thousands of those who are
perishing for want of what they have more than

they can use (the love and saving power of Christ) — how dare such face eternity with those thousands of despairing eyes fixed on them, and those voices ringing in their ears, 'No love . . . no love.' Surely those voices will rise up again at the last day, and accuse such selfishness? The world would accuse anyone so greedy that they will not give their overflow to those who have none — how about the world's God? 'Christ died for ALL.' His love is for *all* — therefore there is more than you or I can use of it. What do we do with the overflow? Do we *pray* it into other lives? Do we give of our money to send it to others? Or have we ever honestly faced the question, 'If I asked, would He free me from circumstances to take it in person to them?'

I looked upon another face — just a girl of twenty — dead before we got to her door, and over that paleness was written that same cry, 'No love . . . no love.' Her home was about to marry her (sell her it really is) into a loveless life. She evidently knew the future it would hold for her, and couldn't face it. All day she worked embroidery on her wedding shoes, determining (what thoughts for a young girl with life all ahead of her) that they should be her shroud, and at eveningtide she quietly took poison. They were putting those shoes on her dead feet when we arrived, and they told me, crying bitterly, 'She has always been such a good girl!' Perhaps there are others 'working on their shrouds' in the purposes of their heart at this very moment, while those who might bring them the Love that enthralled Laddie's heart the first time he heard of it, are sitting at home, putting in time over puny nothings, regardless of that bitter cry that comes over the sea to them — 'No love . . . no love.'

I said that that little woman laid a scar on our hearts, and I pray that she may lay a scar on many another's too! Perhaps her unconscious message and rebuke will save many thousands of her fellow sisters, if you who read this will but stand up and join the 'Second-Mile People'.

'For grace alone can reach me,
And love alone can win.'

'Oh when we are dying,
How glad we will be,
That the lamp of our life
Has been burned out for Thee!'

OTHER BOOKS BY ISOBEL KUHN

ASCENT TO THE TRIBES
Abridgement of Isobel Kuhn's classic story of pioneer missionary work among the tribespeople of North Thailand.

BY SEARCHING
An autobiography with a difference — remarkable for its honesty and frankness. The story of one person's search for God and her obedience as she found Him.

GREEN LEAF IN DROUGHT
The poignant story of *Rupert Clarke* and *Arthur Mathews*, the last CIM missionaries released from Communist China after two years in captivity.

IN THE ARENA
This continuation of the best-selling autobiography *By Searching* tells of Isobel Kuhn's call to China and many years of work there with her husband.

NESTS ABOVE THE ABYSS
A vivid description of the work of the Holy Spirit among the Lisu people of south-west China.

STONES OF FIRE
A true story about Mary, a young Lisu tribeswoman living in the Salween canyon in south-west China. A sober account of God's intervention which can be relied upon in any hour of trial.